Arts And Crafts For Little Hands

Pre-K–Grade 1

Compiled By:
Jennifer L. Overend

Editors:
Ada Hamrick
Jennifer L. Overend
Amanda Wheeler

Copy Editors:
Carol Rawleigh, Gina Sutphin

Illustrators:
Jennifer T. Bennett, Cathy Spangler Bruce, Donna K. Teal

Editorial Assistant:
Carol LaJeunesse

Typographer:
Lynette Maxwell

Cover Design:
Donna K. Teal

Table Of Contents

How To Use This Book:

Arts and crafts for your little ones have never been easier! Each project in this book features a key to the level of difficulty, the skills involved, a materials list, an illustration of the completed project, teacher preparation hints, student steps, and finishing touches.

Three hands in an upper corner of each page make it easy to determine the level of difficulty for each project.

This is an easy project requiring minimum fine motor skills or simple cutting. Appropriate for young learners.

This project is of moderate difficulty, requiring more intricate cutting or handling of small pieces.

This project is more involved and will require more highly developed fine motor skills and the ability to complete several steps.

You will see a series of icons at the top of each page, indicating the skills involved in the project.

Drawing Coloring

Painting (using paint or a paintbrush)

Gluing

Cutting

Tracing

Tying

Fine Motor Skills (This includes handling small objects, stringing, sewing, or using hand strength and coordination.)

 The teacher icon may appear in the "Student Steps" section. This indicates that some adult assistance or supervision may be required with one or more of the steps.

Falling Leaves

Materials:
(for one project)

1/2 sheet of 9" x 12" brown
    construction paper
sheet of 9" x 12"
    construction paper
several 1" construction-
    paper squares
glue
scissors

Preparation Hints:

1. Cut brown construction paper
   into 1/2 sheets.
2. Cut several sheets of fall-colored
   construction paper into squares.

Student Steps:

1. Cut a tree trunk from the 1/2
   sheet of brown construction
   paper.
2. Glue the trunk to the 9" x 12"
   sheet of construction paper.
3. Glue the squares to the top of the
   tree trunk and below to represent
   leaves.
4. Allow the glue to dry.

Finishing Touches:

1. Display the finished projects on a
   bulletin board titled "Falling
   Leaves."
2. For a math activity, have children
   count the number of squares
   used on their pictures.

Anne M. Cromwell-Gapp—Gr. Pre-K,
Keene Day Care Center,
Keene, NH

Squeeze-A-Tree

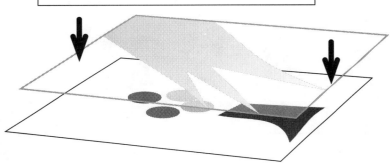

Materials:

(for one project)

12" x 18" sheet of light-
   colored construction paper
1/2 sheet of 9" x 12" brown
   construction paper
tempera paint (brown, yellow,
   red, orange)
12" x 18" sheet of waxed
   paper
newspaper
glue

Preparation Hints:

1. Collect newspaper.
2. Fill small squeeze bottles with paint.

Student Steps:

1. Cover the work surface with newspaper.
2. Tear a tree trunk from the brown construction paper and glue it to the bottom of the large sheet as shown.
3. Squeeze a small amount (quarter-size) of each color of paint above the tree trunk.
4. Place waxed paper over the entire picture and press down on the paint so the colors mix together.
5. Leave in place overnight.

Finishing Touches:

1. Remove the waxed paper from the picture. (Bits of waxed paper may stick to the paint and help create a soft sheen.)
2. Display students' artwork with an autumn poem.

Outline Leaves

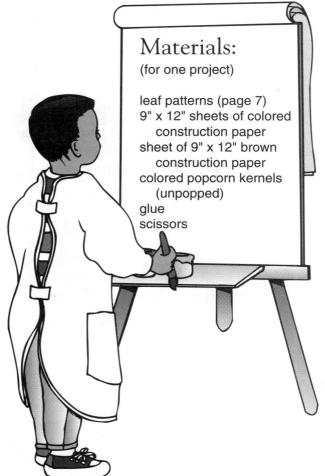

Materials:
(for one project)

leaf patterns (page 7)
9" x 12" sheets of colored
    construction paper
sheet of 9" x 12" brown
    construction paper
colored popcorn kernels
    (unpopped)
glue
scissors

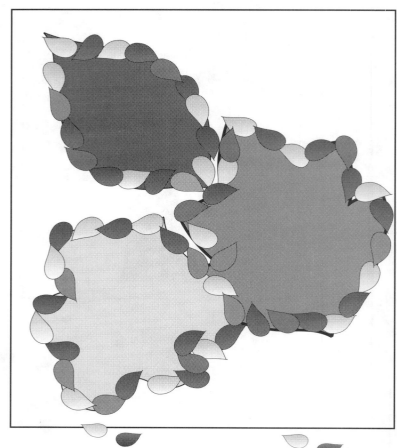

Preparation Hints:

1. Purchase a bag of colored popcorn kernels.
2. Duplicate the leaf patterns on several sheets of colored construction paper.
3. Cut the leaf patterns apart.

Student Steps:

1. Cut out three different colored leaf patterns.
2. Glue the leaf patterns to the brown construction paper.
3. Glue the colored popcorn along the edges of the leaves.
4. Allow the glue to dry.

Finishing Touches:

1. Display the completed projects on a bulletin board titled "Our Autumn Forest."

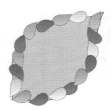

Note: Teacher will cut the leaves apart before giving several different colored leaves to each student.

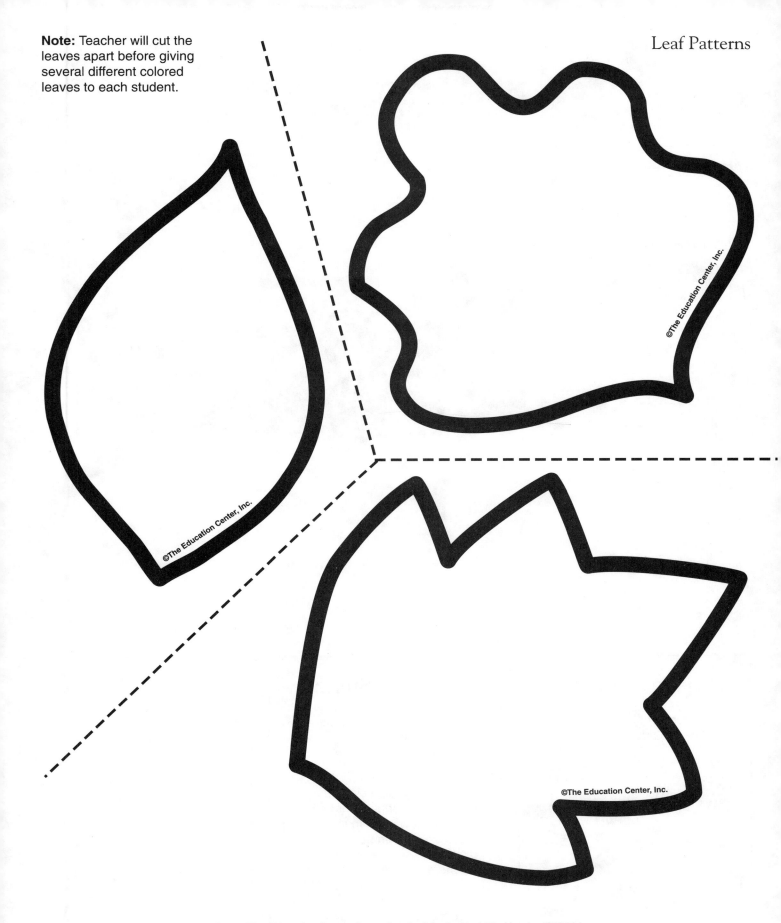

©The Education Center, Inc.

©The Education Center, Inc.

©The Education Center, Inc.

Spool Spider

Materials:
(for one project)

wooden spool
black tempera paint
4 black pipe cleaners
2 wiggle eyes
glue
paintbrush

Preparation Hints:

1. Purchase spools, pipe cleaners, and wiggle eyes at a craft store.

Student Steps:

Session 1:
1. Paint the spool with the black tempera paint.
2. Allow the paint to dry.

Session 2:
1. Push the four pipe cleaners through the spool so that equal lengths show on both sides. Squeeze glue on both sides of the hole to secure the pipe cleaners and allow to dry.
2. Arrange the spider legs in the desired positions.
3. Glue the wiggle eyes to the spider as shown.

Finishing Touches:

1. Display the spiders on a bulletin board with imitation spiderweb material.
2. Read *Be Nice To Spiders* by Margaret B. Graham and display the spiders in a reading corner.

Ghost In A Bag

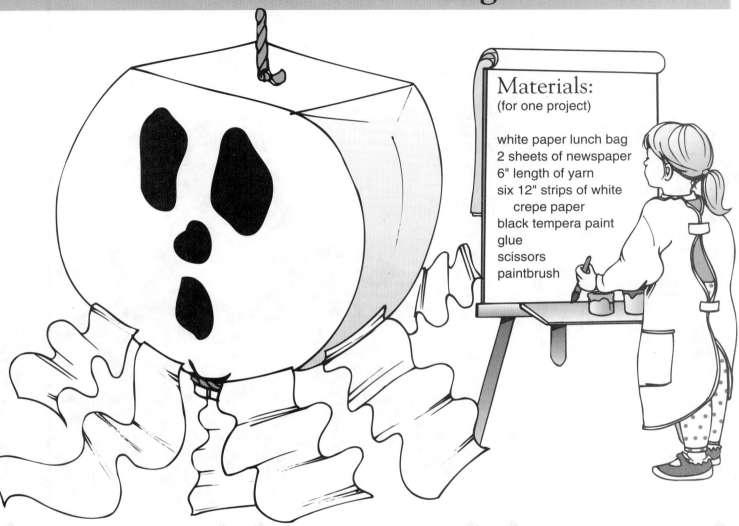

Materials:
(for one project)

white paper lunch bag
2 sheets of newspaper
6" length of yarn
six 12" strips of white
   crepe paper
black tempera paint
glue
scissors
paintbrush

Preparation Hints:

1. Provide lunch bags and crepe paper.
2. Collect newspaper.
3. Cut yarn and crepe paper into necessary lengths.

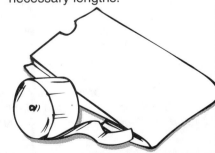

Student Steps:

1. Stuff the lunch bag with newspaper.
2. Twist the top and tie with the yarn.
3. Cut the gathered section off the bag.
4. Paint a ghost face on the bag.
5. Glue the crepe-paper strips to the base of the ghost.

Finishing Touches:

1. Tie a length of yarn to the top of the project and suspend from the ceiling for a flying ghost!
2. Or read *Georgie* by Robert Bright and use the ghosts to decorate your reading area.

*Carmen Sortino—Gr. Pre-K,
The College Of Staten Island's
Children's Center, Staten Island, NY*

FALL

Halloween Witch

Materials:

(for one project)
paper lunch bag
6" length of yarn
tempera paint (green and
   black)
4" strips of black crepe paper
2 sheets of 9" x 12" black
   construction paper
newspaper
glue
scissors
paintbrush
stapler

Preparation Hints:

1. Provide lunch bags and crepe paper.
2. Collect newspaper.
3. Cut yarn and crepe paper into necessary lengths.
4. Cut nine-inch circles from black construction paper; then cut a star shape into the center of each. (See Session 2, Step 3.)

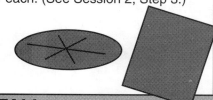

Student Steps:

Session 1:
1. Stuff the paper bag with crumpled newspaper.
2. Tie the bag closed and cut off the excess paper.
3. Paint the bag green and allow to dry.

Session 2:
1. Use black paint to make witch facial features.
2. Glue several crepe-paper strips to the bag for hair.
3. To make a hat, roll one piece of black construction paper into a cone and staple it. Insert the cone into the prepared construction-paper circle.
4. Glue the brim to the hat and the hat to the bag.

Finishing Touches:

1. Attach strings to the gathered tops of the bags and suspend the witches from the ceiling.

*Carmen Sortino—Gr. Pre-K,
The College Of Staten Island's
Children's Center, Staten Island, NY*

"Marble-ous" Web

Materials:
(for one project)

9" black construction-
  paper circle
9" round cake pan
5 or 6 marbles
white tempera paint
plastic spider
glue

Preparation Hints:

1. Purchase plastic spiders.
2. Collect marbles and cake pans.
3. Cut black construction paper into nine-inch circles.

Student Steps:

Session 1:
1. Place the construction-paper circle into the cake pan.
2. Dip the marbles in white paint and place them in the cake pan.
3. Tilt the pan to make the marbles roll around.
4. Remove the marbles and allow the paint to dry.

Session 2:
1. Remove the paper from the pan and glue a plastic spider to the web.

Finishing Touches:

1. If desired, attach each spider to a thread and suspend it from the bottom of its web.

Ann Scalley—Gr. Pre-K,
Wellfleet Preschool,
Wellfleet, MA

Rice Jack-O'-Lantern

Materials:
(for one project)

handful of white rice
decorative dye (page 156)
6" paper plate
1/4 sheet of 9" x 12" black
  construction paper
green construction-paper
  scraps
glue
scissors

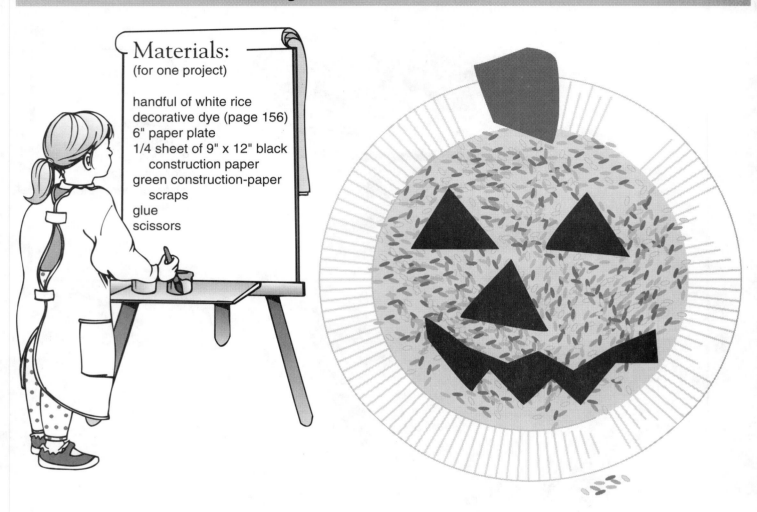

Preparation Hints:

1. Provide rice and paper plates.
2. Using the decorative dye, color
   the rice orange and allow to dry.
3. Cut black construction paper into
   one-fourth sheets.

Student Steps:

1. Spread a coat of glue on the
   paper plate and sprinkle the rice
   on top.
2. Cut jack-o'-lantern features from
   the black construction paper and
   a stem from the green scraps.
3. Glue the cutouts on top of the rice
   and allow to dry.

Finishing Touches:

1. Display the finished projects with
   a Halloween poem.
2. Or have children use their jack-o'-
   lanterns while reciting the
   fingerplay "Five Little Pumpkins
   Sitting On A Gate."

*Beth Schimmel—Gr. Pre-K,
Blue Ridge Elementary,
Pinetop, AZ*

Whiskers The Cat

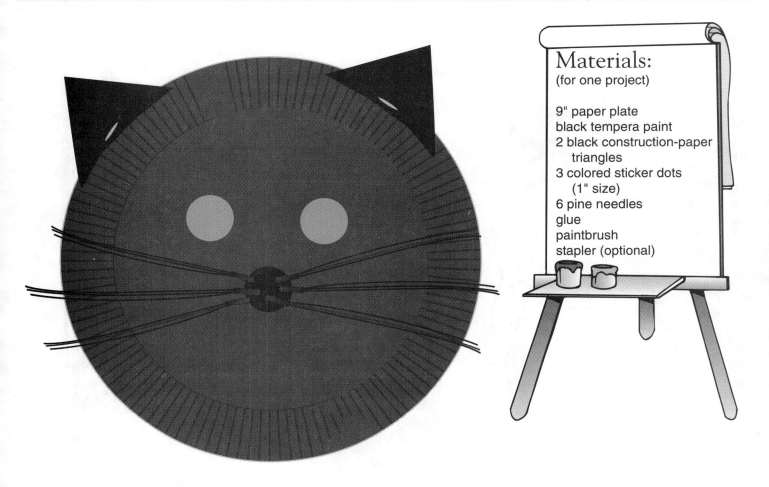

Materials:
(for one project)

9" paper plate
black tempera paint
2 black construction-paper
   triangles
3 colored sticker dots
   (1" size)
6 pine needles
glue
paintbrush
stapler (optional)

Preparation Hints:

1. Provide paper plates and sticker dots.
2. Collect or purchase pine needles.
3. Cut triangular ears from black construction paper.

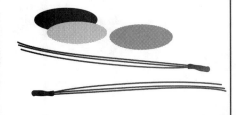

Student Steps:

Session 1:
1. Paint one side of the paper plate black and allow to dry.

Session 2:
1. Attach the triangles to the paper plate using glue (or staples) to make cat ears.
2. Use the sticker dots to give the cat two eyes and a nose.
3. Glue three pine needles on each side of the nose to make whiskers.

Finishing Touches:

1. Display the finished projects on a Halloween-theme bulletin board titled "Black Cat Buddies."

*Beth Schimmel—Gr. Pre-K,
Blue Ridge Elementary,
Pinetop, AZ*

Spider House

Materials:

(for one project)
house pattern (page 15)
8 1/2" x 11" sheets of
    tagboard
9" x 12" sheet of black
    construction paper
white tempera paint
2" length of black yarn
small plastic spider
small ghost-shaped
    sponges
white crayon
scissors
stapler

Preparation Hints:

1. Purchase plastic spiders.
2. Duplicate several copies of the house pattern on tagboard and cut them out for use as templates.
3. Cut black yarn into two-inch lengths.
4. Prepare small ghost-shaped sponges for painting (see the "Finicky Fingers" technique on page 157).

Student Steps:

Session 1:
1. Trace the house template on black construction paper. Cut it out.
2. Cut and fold a door as shown.
3. Draw windows with the white crayon.
4. Sponge-paint the house with white tempera ghosts and allow it to dry.

Session 2:
1. Tie the yarn to the spider.
2. Staple the yarn to the house, suspending the spider from the doorway as shown.

Finishing Touches:

1. Display the finished projects in a reading corner along with the book *The Very Busy Spider* by Eric Carle.

Adapted from an idea by Lori Pieper—Gr. 2, Mirage Elementary, Phoenix, AZ

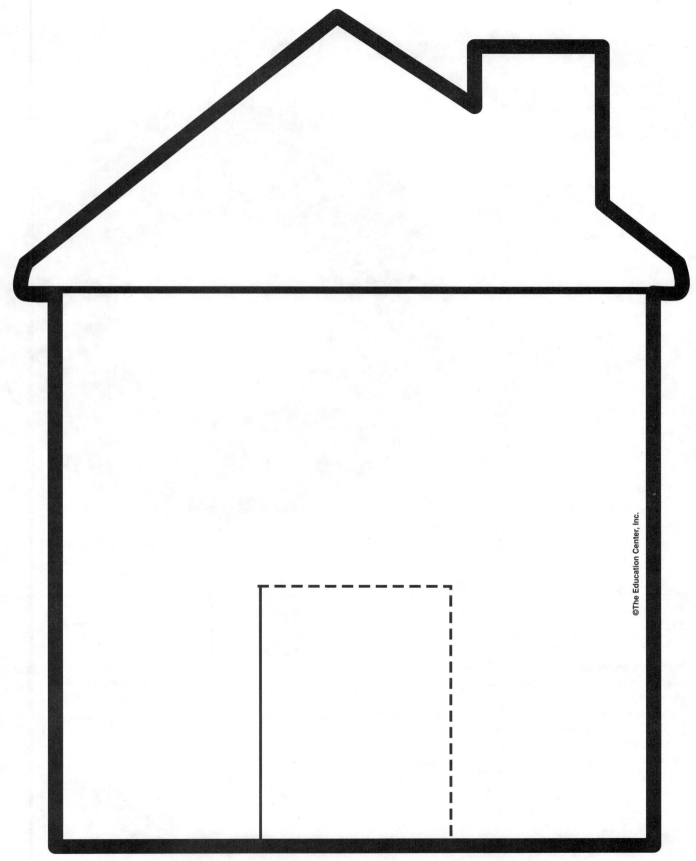

©1995 The Education Center, Inc. • *Arts And Crafts For Little Hands* • TEC891

FALL

Autumn Wreath

Materials:
(for one project)

9" paper plate
brown tempera paint
several fall leaves
small pinecones
glue
paintbrush
scissors

Preparation Hints:

1. Provide paper plates.
2. Gather fall leaves and small pinecones.
3. Punch a hole in the center of each plate as a starting point for cutting. (Or, if desired, cut out the entire center of each plate for younger students.)

Student Steps:

Session 1:
1. Cut out the center of the paper plate.
2. Paint the outer rim of the plate brown; then allow it to dry.

Session 2:
1. Arrange several autumn leaves and some small pinecones on the wreath and glue them in place.

Finishing Touches:

1. Have children take the wreaths home to use as door decorations.
2. Display the wreaths in classroom windows.

Corny Napkin Ring

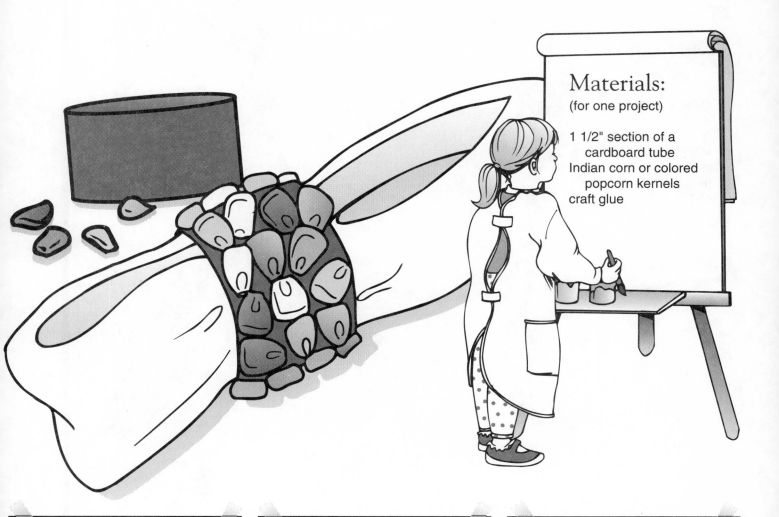

Materials:
(for one project)

1 1/2" section of a
  cardboard tube
Indian corn or colored
  popcorn kernels
craft glue

Preparation Hints:

1. Provide Indian corn or colored popcorn kernels and craft glue. (Craft glue is thicker and tackier than school glue.)
2. Collect and cut cardboard tubes into 1 1/2" sections.

Student Steps:

1. Glue the Indian corn or colored popcorn kernels to the outside of the cardboard ring.
2. Allow the glue to dry.

Finishing Touches:

1. Have students use these napkin rings in class for a Thanksgiving celebration.
2. Or have each child make several napkin rings to give to family members.

Terrific Tepee

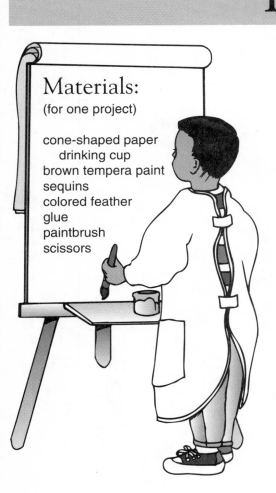

Materials:
(for one project)

cone-shaped paper
   drinking cup
brown tempera paint
sequins
colored feather
glue
paintbrush
scissors

Preparation Hints:

1. Gather drinking cups, sequins, and feathers.

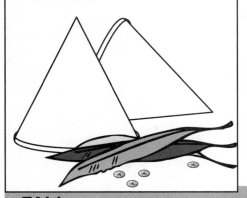

Student Steps:

Session 1:
1. Cut a triangle-shaped door in the cup as shown.
2. Paint the outside of the cup and allow to dry.

Session 2:
1. Decorate the cup by gluing on as many sequins as desired.
2. Glue a colored feather to the top of the tepee.

Finishing Touches:

1. Display the finished tepees in a reading corner. Share a story about the Native Americans of the Plains, such as *The Legend Of The Indian Paintbrush* by Tomie De Paola.

Beth Schimmel—Gr. Pre-K,
Blue Ridge Elementary,
Pinetop, AZ

Pinecone Turkey

©The Education Center, Inc.

©The Education Center, Inc.

Materials:
(for one project)

patterns at left
sheet of 9" x 12" light brown
   construction paper
medium-sized pinecone
crayons
glue
scissors

Preparation Hints:

1. Collect pinecones.
2. Duplicate the head and tail patterns on light brown construction paper.

Student Steps:

1. Cut out the turkey head and tail patterns.
2. Use crayons to color the head and tail.
3. Glue the cutouts to the pinecone as shown. Hold the cutouts in place while the glue dries.

Finishing Touches:

1. Have children take the turkeys home as decorations for Thanksgiving.
2. Or use the turkeys as table decorations in your school cafeteria.

FALL

Turkey On A Plate

Materials:
(for one project)

turkey patterns (page 21)
9" paper plate
sheet of 9" x 12" brown
    construction paper
crayons
glue
scissors

Preparation Hints:

1. Purchase paper plates.
2. Cut out a small section of each paper-plate rim as shown. Save the cut-out pieces for the students to use in Step 5.
3. Duplicate copies of the turkey head and feet patterns onto brown construction paper.

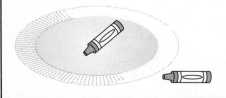

Student Steps:

1. Cut out the duplicated head and feet.
2. Glue the head onto the center of the paper plate as shown.
3. Glue the feet to the back of the paper plate.
4. Color the remaining rim of the paper plate.
5. Color two reserved pieces of paper-plate rim and glue them to the turkey body for wings.

Finishing Touches:

1. Display the finished turkeys on a Thanksgiving-theme bulletin board titled "Turkeys Galore!"

Adapted from an idea by Mary E. Maurer—Gr. Pre-K, Caddo, OK

©The Education Center, Inc.

©The Education Center, Inc.

©1995 The Education Center, Inc. • *Arts And Crafts For Little Hands* • TEC891

FALL

Handy Shadow Turkey

Materials:
(for one project)

overhead projector
1/2 sheet of 9" x 12" brown
   construction paper
sheet of unlined chart paper
tape
crayons
scissors

Preparation Hints:

1. Cut brown construction paper into 1/2 sheets.
2. Set up the overhead projector.
3. Tape the chart paper to the wall and shine the projector onto it.

Student Steps:

1. Place your hand on the overhead projector as an adult traces around the outline on the chart paper.
2. Use crayons to color the outline and add turkey features as shown.
3. Cut legs and feet from brown construction paper.
4. Tape the legs to the back of the turkey.

Finishing Touches:

1. Display the finished projects with the title "Great Gobblers."
2. Or decorate your reading area with the turkeys and read *A Turkey For Thanksgiving* by Eve Bunting.

Mary Langford—Gr. K,
St. Agnes School,
Butler, WI

Glue-A-Greeting Magnet

I LOVE SANTA

JOSH

Materials:
(for one project)

craft stick
tempera paint
alphabet pasta
decorative dye (page 156)
magnetic tape
glue
paintbrush

Preparation Hints:

1. Purchase a box of alphabet pasta, craft sticks, and magnetic tape.
2. Cut the magnetic tape into pieces.
3. If desired, color the alphabet pasta using decorative dye.

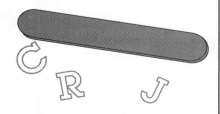

Student Steps:

Session 1:
1. Paint the craft stick and allow it to dry.

Session 2:
1. Choose a holiday message and find the appropriate alphabet-pasta letters.
2. Glue the letters onto the craft stick.

Finishing Touches:

1. Attach a piece of magnetic tape to the back of the craft stick.
2. Have each child present it to a family member as a gift.

*Jennifer A. Milo,
Troy, NY*

DONNA

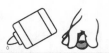

Fancy Photo Ornament

Materials:
(for one project)

1/2 of a 3" foam ball
decorative items such as:
   sequins, plastic jewels,
   beads
pipe-cleaner half
student photo
glue

Preparation Hints:

1. Purchase foam balls, decorative items, and pipe cleaners.
2. Cut the foam balls and pipe cleaners into halves.
3. Collect student photos.

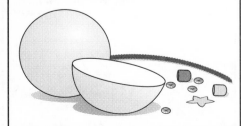

Student Steps:

1. Glue the photo to the flat side of the foam ball.
2. Decorate the foam ball by gluing on decorative items.
3. Push the pipe-cleaner half into the top of the ornament and secure it with a few drops of glue. Shape the pipe cleaner into a hook.

Finishing Touches:

1. Hang the finished ornaments on a classroom tree.
2. Or let students take them home to add to their family trees.

Adapted from an idea by Janet Keyser Carnes—Gr. K, K. W. Bergan School, Browning, MT

Pretty Pasta Hang-Ups

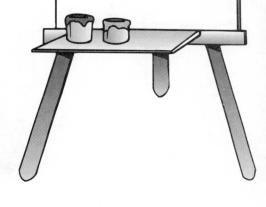

Materials:
(for one project)

pasta (various kinds)
decorative dye (page 156)
3" construction-paper circle
6" length of yarn
glue
hole puncher

Preparation Hints:

1. Provide several kinds of pasta.
2. Color the pasta using decorative dye.
3. Cut three-inch circles from colored construction paper.
4. Cut six-inch lengths of yarn.

Student Steps:

1. Use the hole puncher to punch a hole in the construction-paper circle.
2. Thread the length of yarn through the hole and tie it to create a loop.
3. Glue the pasta pieces to the circle.

Finishing Touches:

1. Suspend the finished ornaments in classroom windows.
2. Or send the ornaments home to be used as holiday decorations.

WINTER

Christmas Candy Cane

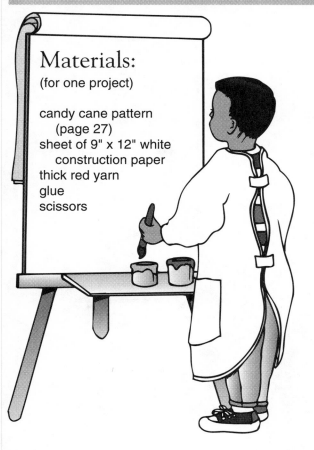

Materials:
(for one project)

candy cane pattern
   (page 27)
sheet of 9" x 12" white
   construction paper
thick red yarn
glue
scissors

Preparation Hints:

1. Provide thick red yarn.
2. Duplicate the candy cane pattern on white construction paper for each child.

Student Steps:

1. Cut out the candy cane pattern.
2. Cut several pieces of red yarn for stripes.
3. Glue the yarn pieces onto the candy cane cutout.

Finishing Touches:

1. Use the completed candy canes as a border for a Christmas bulletin board.
2. Or display in classroom windows as sweet holiday decorations.

Anne M. Cromwell-Gapp—Gr. Pre-K,
Keene Day Care Center,
Keene, NH

WINTER

26

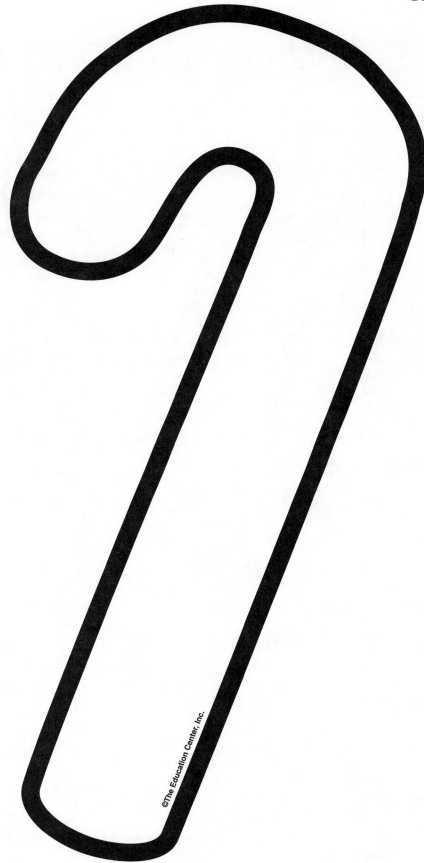

©The Education Center, Inc.

WINTER

3-D Cookie-Cutter Ornament

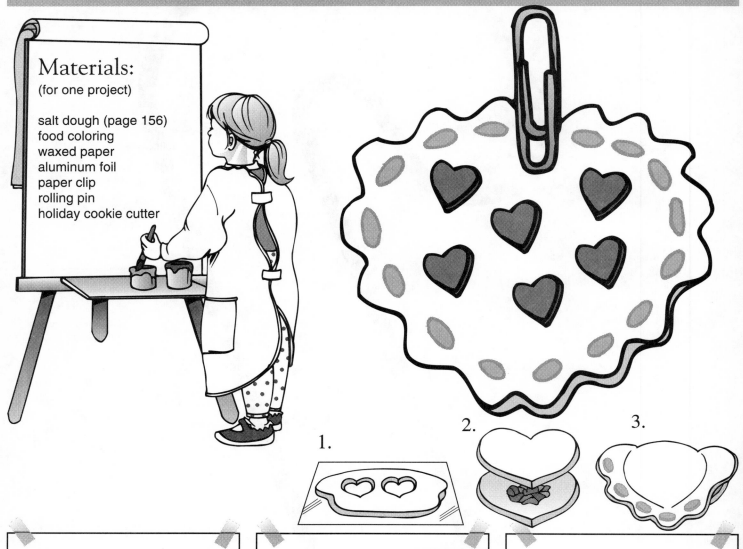

Materials:
(for one project)

salt dough (page 156)
food coloring
waxed paper
aluminum foil
paper clip
rolling pin
holiday cookie cutter

1.

2.

3.

Preparation Hints:

1. Make a batch of salt dough, divide it, and color as desired.
2. Collect rolling pins, cookie cutters, aluminum foil, and paper clips.

Student Steps:

1. Spread waxed paper on top of the work surface.
2. Roll the dough to a thickness of about one-fourth inch.
3. Using a cookie cutter, cut two identical shapes in the dough.
4. Crumple a small amount of aluminum foil into a ball, and place it in the center of one of the cut-out shapes.
5. Place the remaining shape on top of the foil ball and pinch the dough edges together to enclose the foil (see illustrations 2 and 3).

6. Decorate the ornament using different colors of salt dough.
7. Press a paper clip into the top of the ornament as shown.

Finishing Touches:

1. Allow the ornament to dry for several days, or accelerate the process by baking in a 325° oven for about 2 hours.
2. Trim a classroom tree with the finished ornaments.

Sparkling Star

Materials:
(for one project)

waxed paper
glitter (various colors)
6" length of yarn
glue

Preparation Hints:

1. Provide several colors of glitter.
2. Cut lengths of yarn.

Student Steps:

Session 1:
1. Spread waxed paper on top of the work surface.
2. Squeeze the glue onto the waxed paper to make a star as shown.
3. Sprinkle the desired colors of glitter onto the glue. Do not shake off the excess glitter.
4. Allow the glue to dry for approximately two days.

Session 2:
1. Peel the ornament off the waxed paper.

2. Thread a length of yarn through the open star and tie it to make a loop.

Finishing Touches:

1. Suspend the finished stars for a celestial ceiling!

WINTER

Man-In-The-Moon Santa

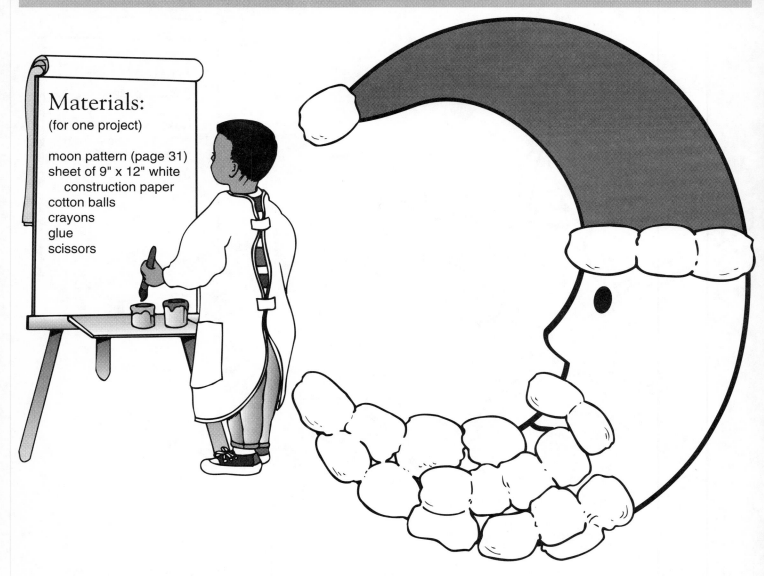

Materials:
(for one project)

moon pattern (page 31)
sheet of 9" x 12" white
    construction paper
cotton balls
crayons
glue
scissors

Preparation Hints:

1. Provide cotton balls.
2. Duplicate the moon pattern on white construction paper for each child.

Student Steps:

1. Cut out the moon pattern.
2. Use crayons to color Santa's hat and facial features.
3. Glue on cotton to make Santa's hat tassel and beard as shown.

Finishing Touches:

1. Display the finished Santas with a Christmas or Santa Claus poem.
2. Or use the Santas as a border for a winter bulletin board.

Theresa L. Moonitz—Gr. K,
P.S. 147 Q,
Cambria Heights, NY

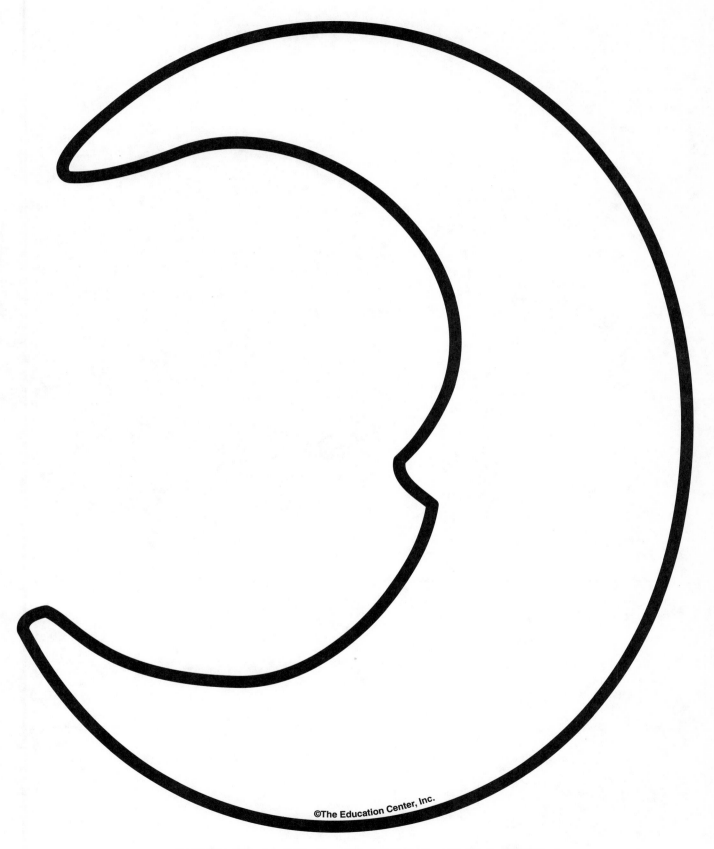

©The Education Center, Inc.

WINTER

Keepsake Ornament

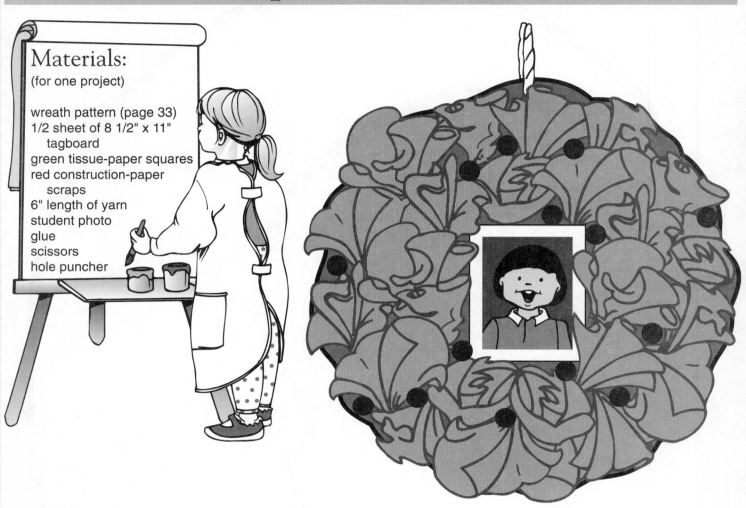

Materials:
(for one project)

wreath pattern (page 33)
1/2 sheet of 8 1/2" x 11"
   tagboard
green tissue-paper squares
red construction-paper
   scraps
6" length of yarn
student photo
glue
scissors
hole puncher

Preparation Hints:

1. Duplicate the wreath pattern on tagboard for each child.
2. Cut green tissue paper into squares.
3. Cut yarn into lengths.
4. Collect student photos or use an instant camera to take photos.

Student Steps:

Session 1:
1. Cut out the wreath pattern.
2. Glue the photo to the center of the wreath.
3. Crumple squares of tissue paper as shown; then glue them to the wreath until covered.
4. Allow the wreath to dry completely.

Session 2:
1. Punch several dots from the red construction-paper scraps.
2. Glue dots to the wreath for berries.

3. Punch a hole in the top of the wreath and tie on a length of yarn.

Finishing Touches:

1. Children can present these special ornaments to parents as holiday gifts.

*Adapted from an idea by
Martha Berry—Gr. Pre-K,
Main Street Methodist Preschool,
Kernersville, NC*

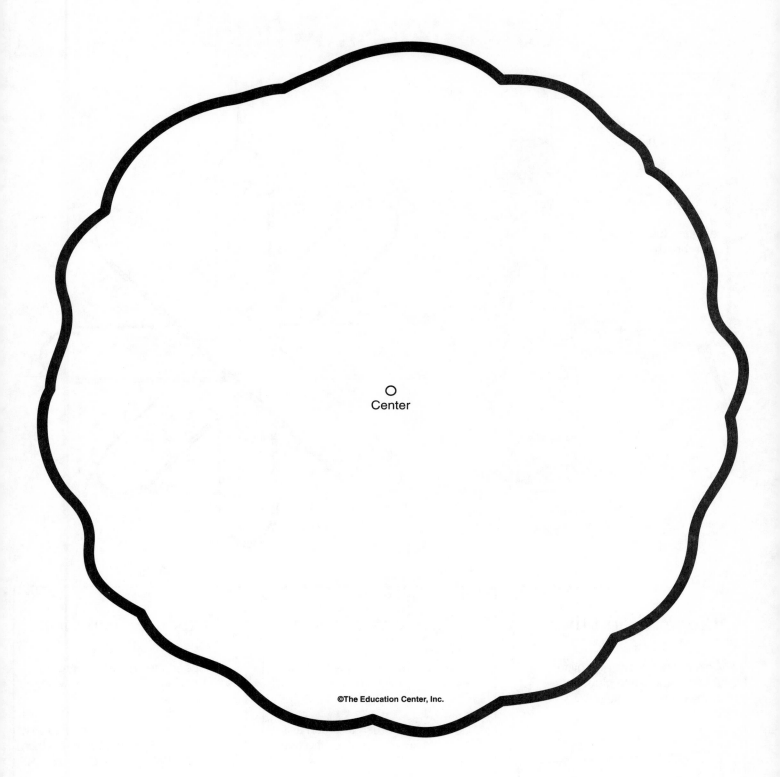

Center

©The Education Center, Inc.

WINTER

Glittering Snowflake

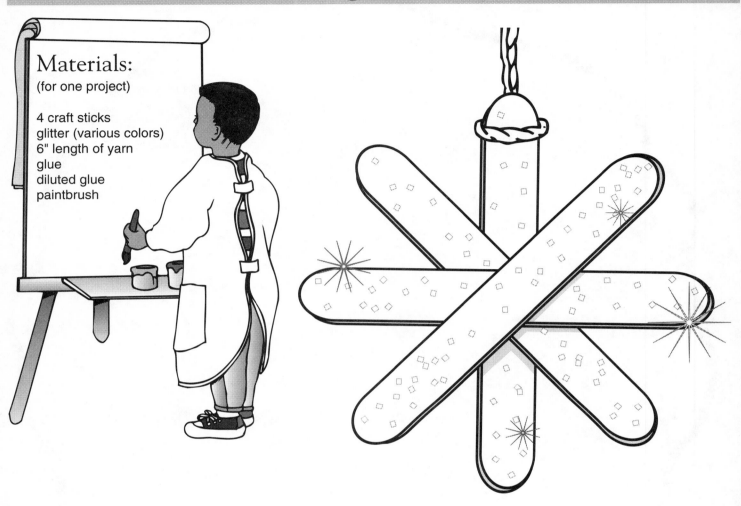

Materials:
(for one project)

4 craft sticks
glitter (various colors)
6" length of yarn
glue
diluted glue
paintbrush

Preparation Hints:

1. Collect craft sticks and glitter.
2. Dilute some white glue.
3. Cut yarn into lengths.

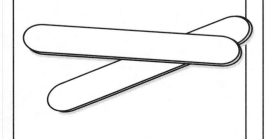

Student Steps:

Session 1:
1. Glue the craft sticks together as shown and allow to dry.

Session 2:
1. Use the paintbrush to brush a coat of diluted glue over the craft sticks.
2. Sprinkle glitter onto the glue. Shake off the excess glitter and allow to dry.
3. Tie the yarn to the completed snowflake, and add a drop of glue to secure.

Finishing Touches:

1. Suspend the snowflakes from the ceiling to create a snowfall to remember!

Jennifer Fry,
Kyrene School District,
Chandler, AZ

Santa Star

Materials:

(for one project)

star pattern (page 133)
sheet of 9" x 12" red
   construction paper
crayons (black and white)
cotton balls
glue
scissors

Preparation Hints:

1. Purchase cotton balls.
2. Duplicate the star pattern on red construction paper for each child.

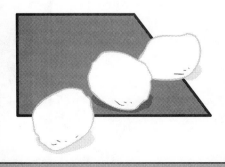

Student Steps:

1. Cut out the star pattern.
2. Use the black crayon to draw a smiling face in the top point of the star.
3. Use the black and white crayons to color the tips of the other four points; then draw a belt across the middle as shown.
4. Glue a small piece of cotton below the face for Santa's beard and another for the top of Santa's hat.

Finishing Touches:

1. Display the finished Santas around the edge of a bulletin board for a colorful holiday border.

*Karen Saner—Grs. K & 1,
Burns Elementary School,
Burns, KS*

WINTER

Snowman Candy Jar

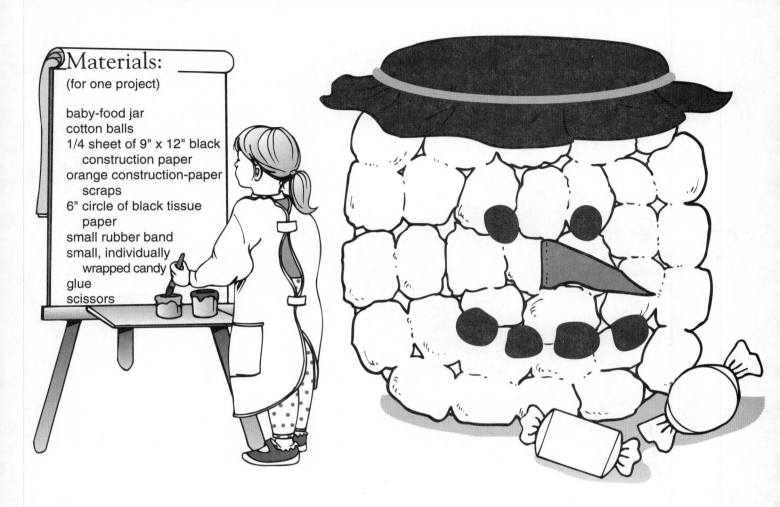

Materials:

(for one project)

baby-food jar
cotton balls
1/4 sheet of 9" x 12" black
   construction paper
orange construction-paper
   scraps
6" circle of black tissue
   paper
small rubber band
small, individually
   wrapped candy
glue
scissors

Preparation Hints:

1. Purchase bags of small, wrapped candies and cotton balls.
2. Collect baby-food jars.
3. Cut black construction paper into one-fourth sheets.
4. Cut six-inch circles from black tissue paper.

Student Steps:

Session 1:
1. Glue cotton balls to the outside of the jar.
2. Cut out eyes and a mouth from black construction paper.
3. Cut out a carrot-shaped nose from the orange construction-paper scraps.
4. Glue the facial features to the cotton-covered jar and let dry.

Session 2:
1. Place the tissue-paper circle on top of the jar opening and

secure it with a small rubber band.

Finishing Touches:

1. Fill the jars with candy and present as gifts to school secretaries, cafeteria workers, or custodial staff.

Adapted from an idea by Suzanne Costner, Maryville, TN

Marshmallow Snowman

Materials:
(for one project)

sheet of 9" x 12" light blue
  construction paper
white minimarshmallows
2 pretzel sticks
crayons
glue

Preparation Hints:

1. Purchase minimarshmallows and pretzel sticks.

Student Steps:

1. Use a white crayon to draw a snowman outline on the construction paper.
2. Color a hat, buttons, and face with crayons.
3. Attach minimarshmallows to the outline by licking the bottom of each minimarshmallow and sticking it to the paper.
4. Glue on pretzel-stick arms.
5. Allow to dry.

Finishing Touches:

1. Eat a few minimarshmallows for a snack while admiring the finished artwork!
2. Use colored marshmallows to create a variety of pictures throughout the year.

Adapted from an idea by Karen Saner—Grs. K & 1, Burns Elementary School, Burns, KS

Frosty Friend

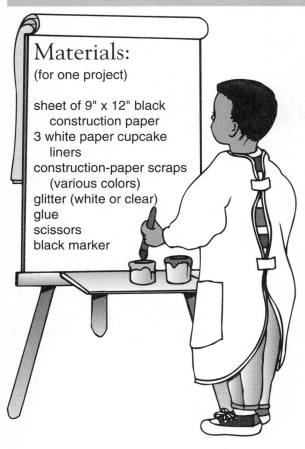

Materials:

(for one project)

sheet of 9" x 12" black
    construction paper
3 white paper cupcake
    liners
construction-paper scraps
    (various colors)
glitter (white or clear)
glue
scissors
black marker

Preparation Hints:

1. Purchase cupcake liners and glitter.

Student Steps:

1. Glue the cupcake liners to the black construction paper as shown.
2. Cut out a hat, mittens, and boots from the construction-paper scraps and glue to the snowman.
3. Use a black marker to draw facial features and buttons.
4. Spread glue around the edges of the cupcake liners and sprinkle on white or clear glitter.

Finishing Touches:

1. Display the snowmen in a reading corner with books such as *The Snowman* by Raymond Briggs and *The Snowman Who Went For A Walk* by Mira Lobe.

*Beth Schimmel—Gr. Pre-K,
Blue Ridge Elementary,
Pinetop, AZ*

Bleeding Heart

Materials:
(for one project)

1" squares of tissue paper
   (various colors)
sheet of 9" x 12" manila
   paper
water
crayon
paintbrush
scissors

Preparation Hints:

1. Cut tissue paper into squares.

Student Steps:

1. Place the tissue-paper squares on the manila paper.
2. Brush water over the squares.
3. Remove the squares, leaving the color behind.
4. After the manila paper dries, trace a heart over the colors and cut it out.

Finishing Touches:

1. Use the hearts as a border for a Valentine's Day bulletin board.
2. Help children write messages or their names on the backs of the hearts and send them home as valentine greetings for parents.

Debra Damiano
Gr. K: Special Education,
Ash Street Center,
Forest Park, GA

Torn-Paper Valentine

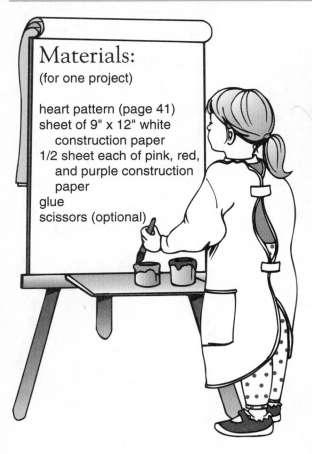

Materials:

(for one project)

heart pattern (page 41)
sheet of 9" x 12" white
  construction paper
1/2 sheet each of pink, red,
  and purple construction
  paper
glue
scissors (optional)

Preparation Hints:

1. Duplicate the heart pattern on white construction paper for each child.
2. Cut colored construction paper into 1/2 sheets.

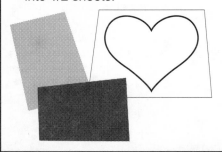

Student Steps:

1. Tear the colored construction paper into small pieces.
2. Spread a coat of glue inside part of the heart outline.
3. Press the torn-paper pieces onto the glue.
4. Continue Steps 2 and 3 until the entire heart is covered.
5. If desired, cut out the heart.

Finishing Touches:

1. Display the finished hearts with a Valentine's Day poem.
2. Or use the hearts to border a February bulletin board.

*Beth Schimmel—Gr. Pre-K,
Blue Ridge Elementary,
Pinetop, AZ*

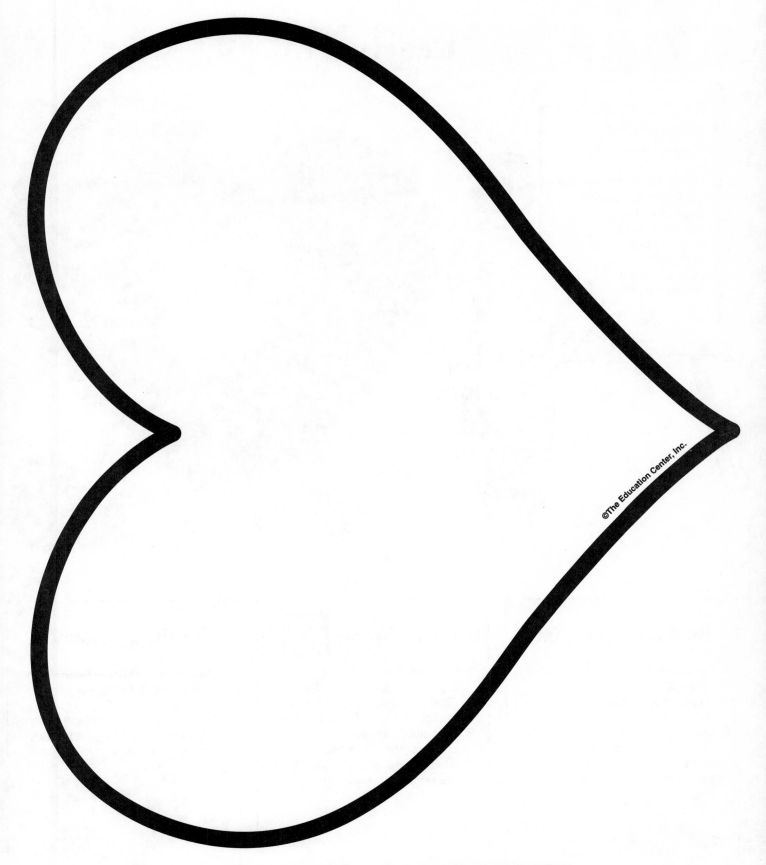

©The Education Center, Inc.

WINTER

Pearly Pin

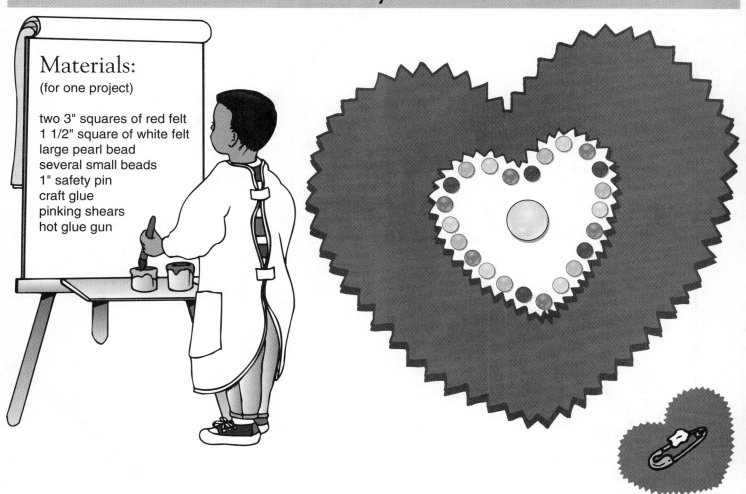

Materials:

(for one project)

two 3" squares of red felt
1 1/2" square of white felt
large pearl bead
several small beads
1" safety pin
craft glue
pinking shears
hot glue gun

Preparation Hints:

1. Purchase the beads, safety pins, and craft glue. (Craft glue is thicker and tackier than school glue.)
2. Use pinking shears to cut large hearts from the three-inch squares of red felt and small hearts from the 1 1/2-inch squares of white felt.

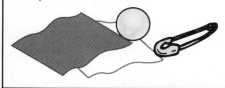

Student Steps:

1. Glue the two red hearts together, aligning the edges.
2. Glue the white heart to the center of one of the red hearts.
3. Glue the pearl bead to the center of the white heart.
4. Glue several small beads along the edge of the white heart.
5. Allow the glue to dry.

Finishing Touches:

1. Attach the safety pin to the back of the project using the hot glue gun.
2. Have children present the pins as Valentine's Day gifts to their mothers or grandmothers.

Rainbow Wind Sock

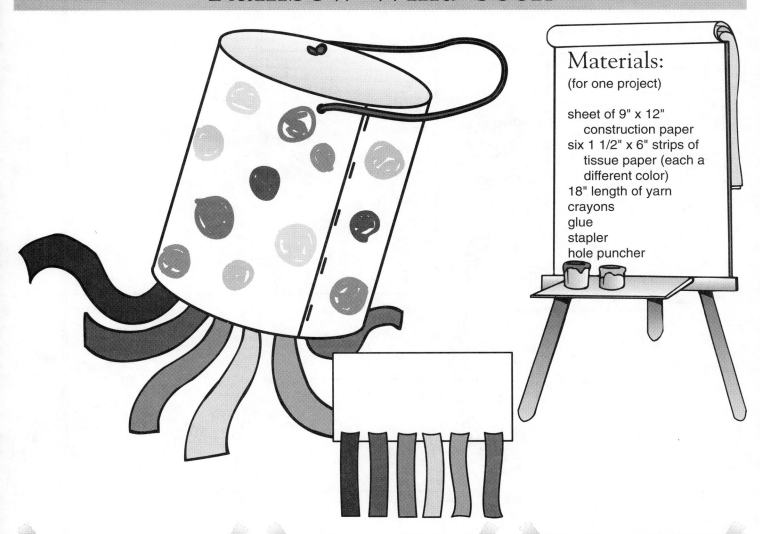

Materials:
(for one project)

sheet of 9" x 12"
   construction paper
six 1 1/2" x 6" strips of
   tissue paper (each a
   different color)
18" length of yarn
crayons
glue
stapler
hole puncher

Preparation Hints:

1. Choose six colors of tissue paper and cut into strips.
2. Cut lengths of yarn.

Student Steps:

1. Color a design on the construction paper.
2. Glue six colored tissue-paper strips in a line across the bottom of the construction paper (see the illustration for Step 2).
3. Roll the construction paper into a cylinder and staple together.
4. Use the hole puncher to punch a hole on opposite sides of the top of the cylinder as shown.
5. Thread the yarn through the holes and tie the ends in a knot.

Finishing Touches:

1. Tie this project into a unit on weather. Have children suspend the wind socks from a fence or tree and discuss changes in the wind.

Anne M. Cromwell-Gapp,
Gr. Pre-K, Keene Day Care Center,
Keene, NH

Speckled Shamrocks

Materials:
(for one project)

shamrock patterns
    (page 45)
2 sheets of 9" x 12" white
    construction paper
several shades of diluted
    green tempera paint
scissors
toothbrush
colander
newspaper

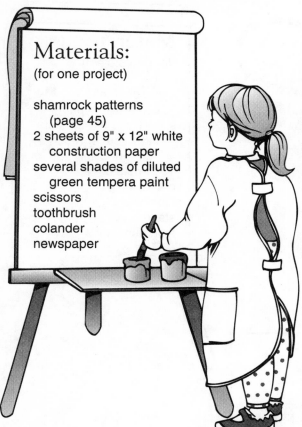

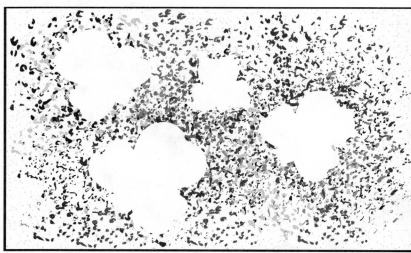

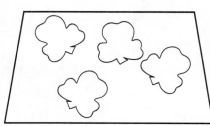

Preparation Hints:

1. Collect a colander, old tooth-brushes, and newspaper.
2. Duplicate the shamrock patterns on white construction paper for each child.
3. Dilute several different shades of green paint and pour into separate containers.

Student Steps:

1. Spread newspaper on top of the work surface.
2. Cut out the shamrocks.
3. Arrange the shamrocks on a sheet of white construction paper.
4. Place the colander over the shamrocks.
5. Dip the toothbrush into one shade of diluted paint and brush it over the colander, making spatter marks.
6. Continue with other shades of green paint.

7. Remove the colander and shamrock patterns from the paper and allow the paint to dry.

Finishing Touches:

1. Display the finished projects on a St. Patrick's Day bulletin board.

SPRING

Darling Daffodil

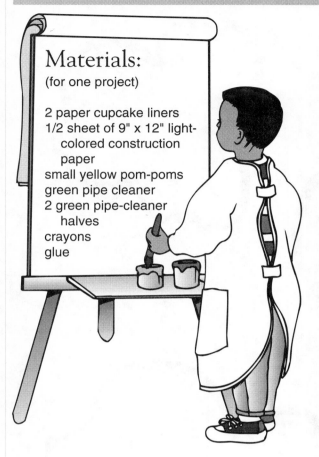

Materials:

(for one project)

2 paper cupcake liners
1/2 sheet of 9" x 12" light-
    colored construction
    paper
small yellow pom-poms
green pipe cleaner
2 green pipe-cleaner
    halves
crayons
glue

Preparation Hints:

1. Collect cupcake liners, pom-poms, and pipe cleaners.
2. Cut construction paper into half sheets.
3. Cut several of the pipe cleaners into halves.

Student Steps:

1. Color one side of each cupcake liner.
2. Position the half sheet of construction paper vertically.
3. Glue one of the cupcake liners (colored side up) to the top of the paper.
4. Place a drop of glue in the center of the first cupcake liner and press on the second cupcake liner (colored side up).
5. Squeeze glue into the center of the top liner and press on a few yellow pom-poms.

6. Gently squeeze the top liner for a 3-D effect.
7. Glue on the green pipe cleaner for a stem.
8. Bend the two pipe-cleaner halves into leaf shapes and glue on each side of the stem.

Finishing Touches:

1. Display the flowers on a bulletin board titled "A Gorgeous Garden."

Anne M. Cromwell-Gapp,
Gr. Pre-K, Keene Day Care Center,
Keene, NH

Magnet Moth

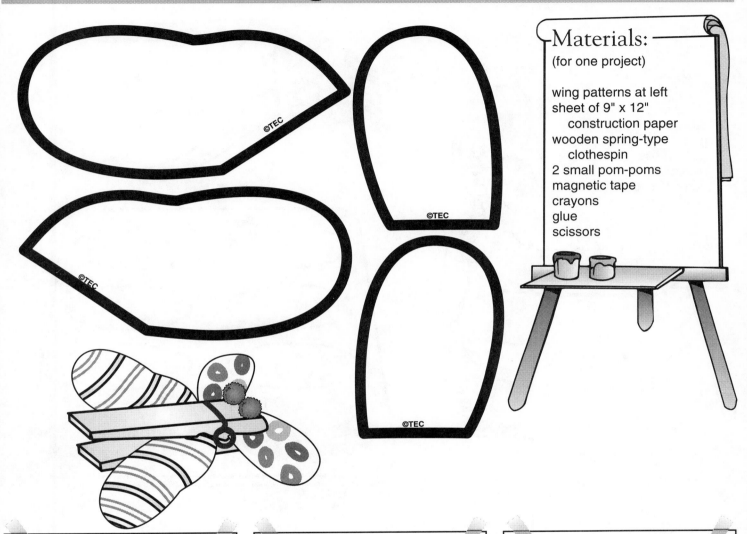

©TEC
©TEC
©TEC
©TEC

Materials:

(for one project)

wing patterns at left
sheet of 9" x 12"
  construction paper
wooden spring-type
  clothespin
2 small pom-poms
magnetic tape
crayons
glue
scissors

Preparation Hints:

1. Purchase clothespins, pom-poms, and magnetic tape.
2. Duplicate the wing patterns on construction paper for each child.
3. Cut the magnetic tape into pieces.

Student Steps:

Session 1:
1. Color the wing patterns; then cut them out.
2. Glue the cutouts on the clothespin as shown.
3. Glue on the pom-poms for eyes and allow to dry.

Session 2:
1. Attach a piece of magnetic tape to the underside of the moth.

Finishing Touches:

1. Use these decorative moths to display student work.
2. Or send each finished magnet home for use on the family refrigerator.

47

Eggs In A Nest

Materials:
(for one project)

salt dough (page 156)
green food coloring
garlic press
muffin tin
nonstick cooking spray
jelly beans

garlic press

Preparation Hints:

1. Purchase cooking spray and jelly beans.
2. Prepare the salt dough and color it green.
3. Collect a garlic press and muffin tins.

Student Steps:

1. Place a small amount of salt dough into the garlic press. Squeeze the press to make salt-dough grass.
2. Spray the muffin tin with non-stick cooking spray.
3. Place a layer of salt-dough grass in the bottom of a muffin-tin cup. Add more grass around the sides and edge.
4. Gently shape the dough into a nest.

Finishing Touches:

1. Allow the salt-dough to harden for several days or accelerate the process by baking in a 325° oven for 1 hour.
2. Cool and remove the nests from the tin.
3. Place jelly beans in each nest.

Beautiful Blossom

Materials:
(for one project)

6" paper plate
9" paper plate
1/2 sheet of 9" x 12"
   green construction
   paper
tempera paint
   (various colors)
glue
scissors
paintbrushes

Preparation Hints:

1. Supply small and large paper plates.

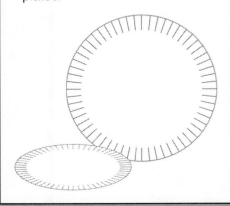

Student Steps:

Session 1:
1. Cut the edges of both paper plates in a wavy fashion to resemble petals as shown.
2. Glue the small plate to the center of the large plate.
3. Allow the glue to dry.

Session 2:
1. Paint the flower and allow to dry.

Session 3:
1. Cut a stem and leaves from the green construction paper.

2. Glue the leaves to the stem and the stem to the blossom.

Finishing Touches:

1. Display the flower blossoms around a bulletin board to create a border bouquet.

SPRING

Mosaic Rainbow

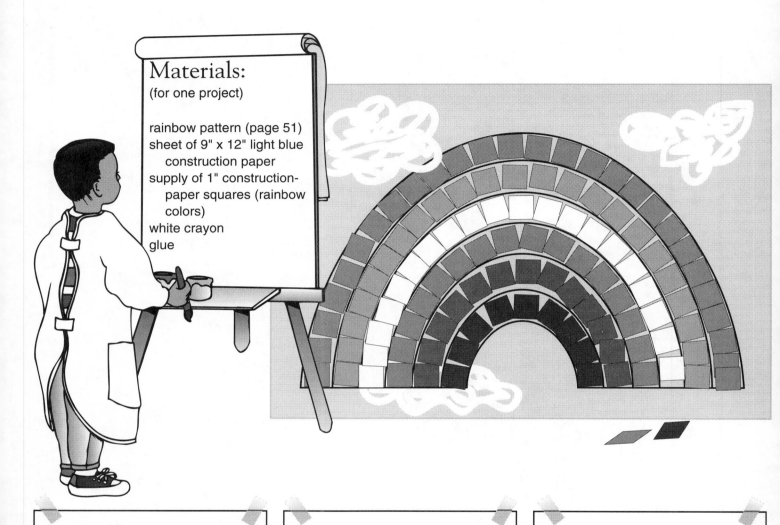

Materials:
(for one project)

rainbow pattern (page 51)
sheet of 9" x 12" light blue
   construction paper
supply of 1" construction-
   paper squares (rainbow
   colors)
white crayon
glue

Preparation Hints:

1. Duplicate the rainbow pattern on light blue construction paper for each child.
2. Cut several sheets of construction paper (red, orange, yellow, green, blue, and purple) into squares.

Student Steps:

1. Spread a coat of glue on the outer arch of the rainbow and press on red squares.
2. Continue with each band of the rainbow, using a different color of squares each time.
3. Color clouds on your paper with a white crayon.

Finishing Touches:

1. Display the finished projects with a rainbow poem.
2. Or display the rainbows in your reading area and read *Skyfire* by Frank Asch.

Sandy Whicker—Gr. Pre-K,
Kernersville Moravian Preschool,
Kernersville, NC

Rainbow Pattern

Wheelbarrow Planter

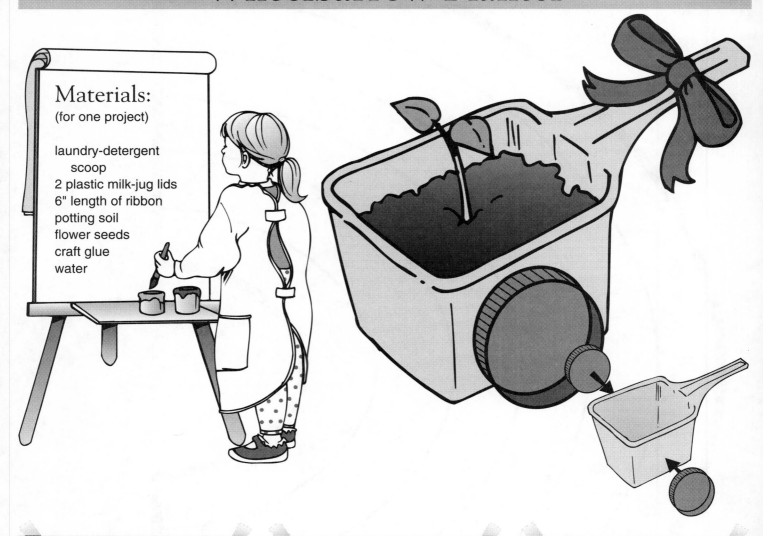

Materials:
(for one project)

laundry-detergent
    scoop
2 plastic milk-jug lids
6" length of ribbon
potting soil
flower seeds
craft glue
water

Preparation Hints:

1. Purchase ribbon, potting soil, flower seeds, and craft glue. (Craft glue is thicker and tackier than school glue.)
2. Collect laundry-detergent scoops and milk-jug lids.
3. Cut ribbon into lengths.

Student Steps:

Session 1:
1. Glue a milk-jug lid to each side of the scoop as shown.
2. Allow the glue to dry.

Session 2:
1. Tie the ribbon to the handle of the scoop.
2. Fill the scoop with potting soil, and plant flower seeds.
3. Sprinkle the soil with a few drops of water.

Finishing Touches:

1. When the plants begin to sprout, send these beautiful spring planters home as gifts.

Kelley Ruffcorn—Gr. K,
South Elementary School,
Modale, IA

Newborns' Nest

Materials:
(for one project)

brown construction-paper
   semicircle
sheet of 9" x 12" light blue
   construction paper
shredded wheat cereal
   (crushed)
2 egg carton sections
colored markers
glue

Preparation Hints:

1. Purchase a box of shredded wheat cereal and crumble the biscuits.
2. Collect and cut apart egg cartons.
3. Cut semicircles from brown construction paper.

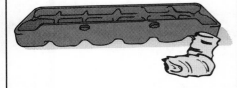

Student Steps:

Session 1:
1. Glue the semicircle to the light blue construction paper as shown.
2. Use a brown marker to draw a tree branch under the nest.
3. Spread a coat of glue on the semicircle and sprinkle crushed cereal on top.
4. Shake off the excess and allow to dry.

Session 2:
1. Draw eyes and a beak on each

egg carton section.
2. Glue the birds on the nest as shown and allow to dry.

Finishing Touches:

1. Display the projects on a bulletin board titled "Welcome Spring!"

*Karen Saner—Grs. K & 1,
Burns Elementary School,
Burns, KS*

SPRING

Pop-Up Butterfly Card

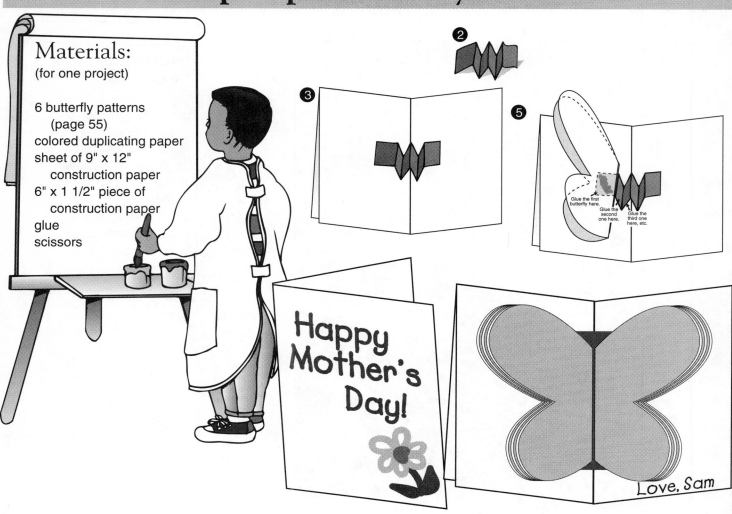

Materials:

(for one project)

6 butterfly patterns
    (page 55)
colored duplicating paper
sheet of 9" x 12"
    construction paper
6" x 1 1/2" piece of
    construction paper
glue
scissors

❸

❷

❺

Glue the first
butterfly here.

Glue the
second
one here.

Glue the
third one
here, etc.

Happy
Mother's
Day!

Love, Sam

Preparation Hints:

1. Duplicate the butterfly patterns on the colored duplicating paper for each child.
2. Cut out 6" x 1 1/2" pieces of construction paper.

Student Steps:

1. Fold the sheet of construction paper in half twice to make a card.
2. Accordion-fold the 6" x 1 1/2" strip into one-inch pleats (see the illustration for Step 2).
3. Glue the outer pleats to the card (see the illustration for Step 3).
4. Cut out the six butterflies.
5. Fold the butterfly cutouts in half vertically and glue two into each accordion pleat (see the illustration for Step 5).

Finishing Touches:

1. Help each child write a message on the front of his card.
2. Children may present the cards for special occasions such as birthdays or Mother's Day.

*Mary E. Maurer—Gr. Pre-K,
Caddo, OK*

©TEC

©TEC

©TEC

©TEC

©TEC

©TEC

SPRING

Wallpaper "Wabbit"

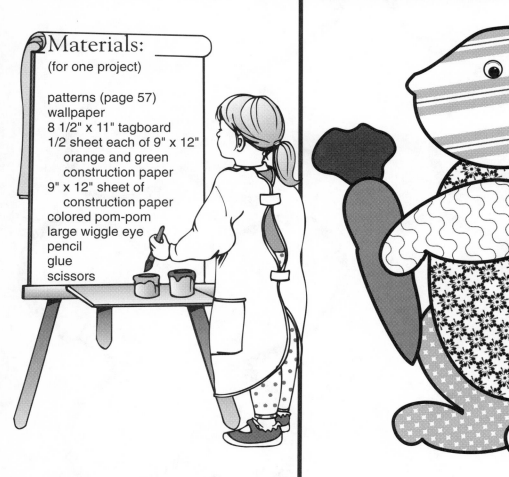

Materials:

(for one project)

patterns (page 57)
wallpaper
8 1/2" x 11" tagboard
1/2 sheet each of 9" x 12"
   orange and green
   construction paper
9" x 12" sheet of
   construction paper
colored pom-pom
large wiggle eye
pencil
glue
scissors

Preparation Hints:

1. Purchase pom-poms and wiggle eyes.
2. Duplicate several copies of the rabbit and carrot patterns on tagboard; then cut them out for use as templates.
3. Cut orange and green construction paper into half sheets.
4. Tear out several wallpaper designs from discarded wallpaper books.

Student Steps:

1. Using the templates, trace and cut out the rabbit body parts from wallpaper.
2. Trace and cut out the carrot from the orange construction paper and the leaves from the green construction paper.
3. Glue the rabbit and carrot patterns on the 9" x 12" sheet of paper as shown.
4. Glue on a wiggle eye and a pom-pom tail.

Finishing Touches:

1. Read *Let's Make Rabbits* by Leo Lionni, and then display the bunnies on a spring or Easter-theme bulletin board.

Cindy Gordon—Gr. K,
Crockett School,
Bryan, TX

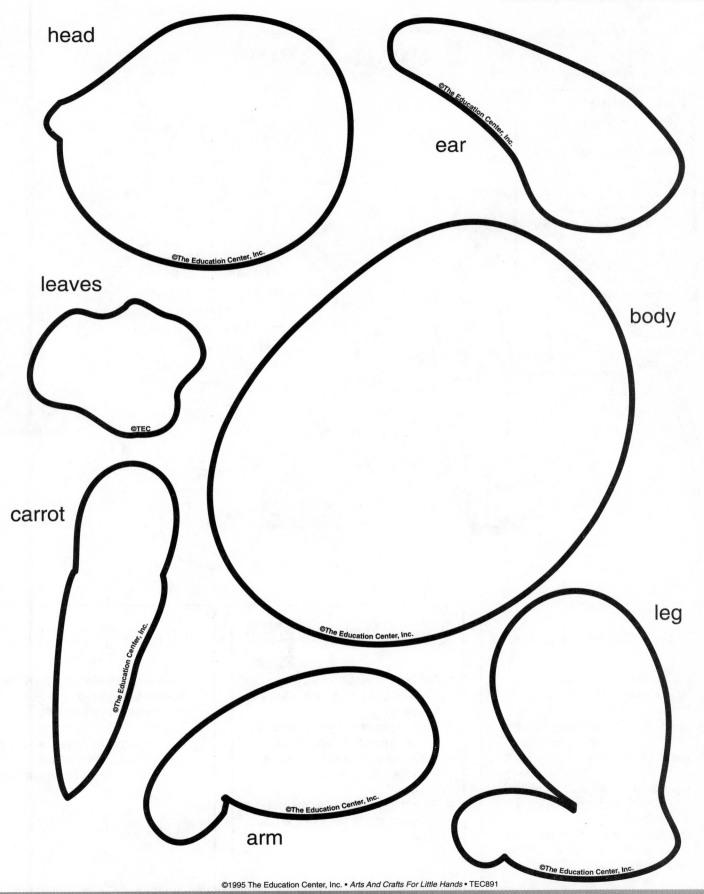

head

ear

leaves

body

carrot

leg

arm

©The Education Center, Inc.

©The Education Center, Inc.

©TEC

©The Education Center, Inc.

©The Education Center, Inc.

©The Education Center, Inc.

©The Education Center, Inc.

Flower Favors

Materials:

(for one project)

petal patterns and poem
  (page 59)
6" paper plate
sheet of 8 1/2" x 11" white
  duplicating paper
sheet of 9" x 12" colored
  construction paper
sheet of 9" x 12" yellow
  construction paper
sheet of 9" x 12" green
  construction paper
glue
scissors
stapler

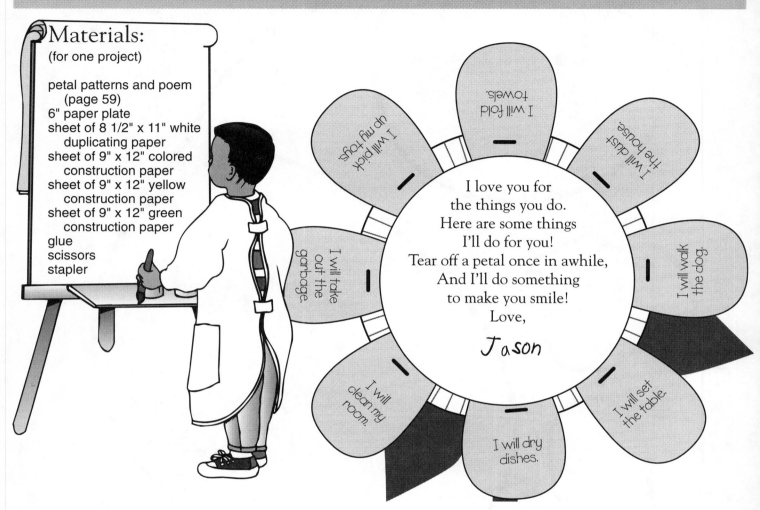

I will fold towels.

I will pick up my toys.

I will dust the house.

I will take out the garbage.

I love you for
the things you do.
Here are some things
I'll do for you!
Tear off a petal once in awhile,
And I'll do something
to make you smile!
Love,
Jason

I will walk the dog.

I will clean my room.

I will dry dishes.

I will set the table.

Preparation Hints:

1. Purchase paper plates.
2. Help children think of eight jobs they can do to help at home.
3. Duplicate two copies of the petal patterns on white duplicating paper and write a different job on each one. Then duplicate the programmed set of eight petals on colored construction paper for each child.
4. Duplicate the poem on page 59 on yellow construction paper for each child.

Student Steps:

1. Cut out the eight petals and staple them around the edge of the paper plate.
2. Cut out the poem and glue it to the center of the paper plate.
3. Cut out a stem and two leaves from the green construction paper.
4. Glue the leaves to the stem. Glue the stem to the back of the paper plate.

Finishing Touches:

1. Have the children give the flowers to their mothers as special Mother's Day gifts.

*Amy Del Vecchio—Gr. K,
Paul Road Elementary School,
Rochester, NY*

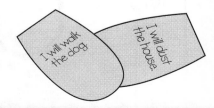

I love you for
the things you do.
Here are some things
I'll do for you!
Tear off a petal once in awhile,
And I'll do something
to make you smile!
Love,

©The Education Center, Inc.

©The Education Center, Inc.

©The Education Center, Inc.

©The Education Center, Inc.

©The Education Center, Inc.

Pot-Scrubber Posy Card

Materials:

(for one project)

poem (page 61)
sheet of 8 1/2" x 11" white
    duplicating paper
colored, plastic pot
    scrubber
sheet of 9" x 12" colored
    construction paper
large brad
green marker
glue

Preparation Hints:

1. Purchase pot scrubbers and brads.
2. Duplicate the poem on white duplicating paper for each child.

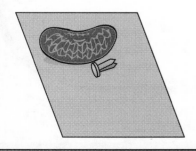

Student Steps:

1. Fold the sheet of construction paper in half to make a card.
2. Place the pot scrubber on the front of the card near the top and fasten it in the center with a brad.
3. Use the green marker to draw a stem and leaves below the scrubber.
4. Glue the poem inside the card.

Finishing Touches:

1. Help children write their names inside the cards and send them home for Mother's Day.

Beverly Provoncha—Gr. Pre-K,
Putnam Central School,
Putnam Station, NY

Happy Mother's Day!

Love,

To make a Mother's Day
gift fantastic,
I drew the stem and leaves
for this flower of plastic.
I give it to Mom
with this special wish...
May it help you scrub
each pot and each dish.

Brite & Clean

ILL NEW!

©TheEducation Center, Inc.

Rockin' Duck

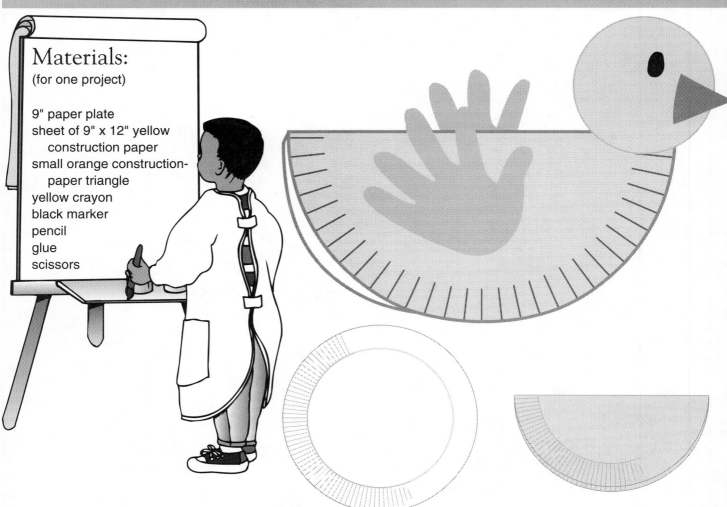

Materials:
(for one project)

9" paper plate
sheet of 9" x 12" yellow
    construction paper
small orange construction-
    paper triangle
yellow crayon
black marker
pencil
glue
scissors

Preparation Hints:

1. Purchase paper plates.
2. Cut small, triangular beaks from orange construction paper.

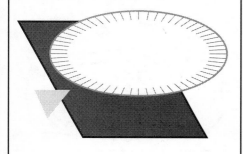

Student Steps:

1. Use a yellow crayon to color one side of the paper plate.
2. Fold the plate in half with the colored side out.
3. Trace two hands on the yellow construction paper and cut them out.
4. Glue a hand cutout to each side of the plate as shown.
5. Cut a circle from yellow construction paper and glue it to the plate for a head.
6. Use the marker to draw an eye on each side of the head.
7. Glue on the orange, triangular beak.
8. Open the paper plate slightly to allow the duck to rock.

Finishing Touches:

1. Set the ducks rocking while singing "Six White Ducks That I Once Knew."

Anne M. Cromwell-Gapp,
Gr. Pre-K, Keene Day Care Center,
Keene, NH

Puff 'n' Paint

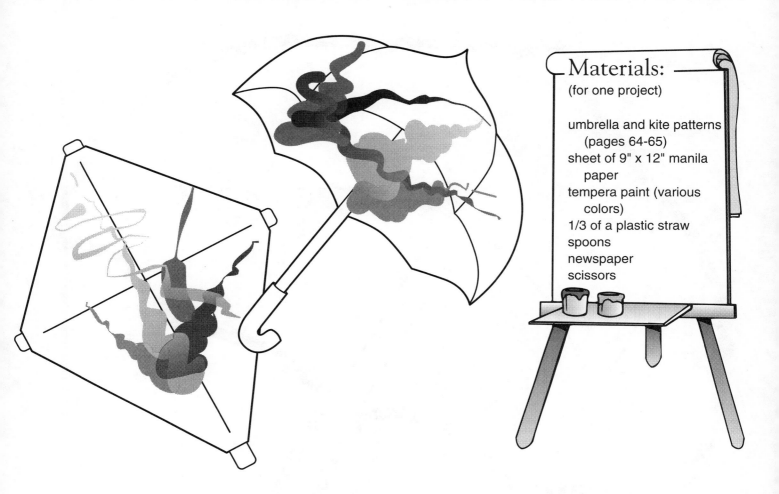

Materials:

(for one project)

umbrella and kite patterns
  (pages 64-65)
sheet of 9" x 12" manila
  paper
tempera paint (various
  colors)
1/3 of a plastic straw
spoons
newspaper
scissors

Preparation Hints:

1. Purchase straws and cut into thirds.
2. Collect spoons and newspaper.
3. Duplicate the umbrella and kite patterns on manila paper.

Student Steps:

1. Cover the work surface with newspaper.
2. Choose a pattern; then cut it out.
3. Lay the pattern on top of the newspaper.
4. Place a spoonful of paint on the pattern.
5. Use the straw to blow the paint in different directions.
6. Repeat Steps 4 and 5 with other paint colors.

Finishing Touches:

1. Use the umbrella and kite patterns to decorate a reading corner displaying the book *Curious George Flies A Kite* by Margaret Rey.
2. Display the finished artwork on a bulletin board titled "Wet-'n'-Windy Weather."

Debra Damiano,
Gr. K: Special Education,
Ash Street Center,
Forest Park, GA

Umbrella Pattern

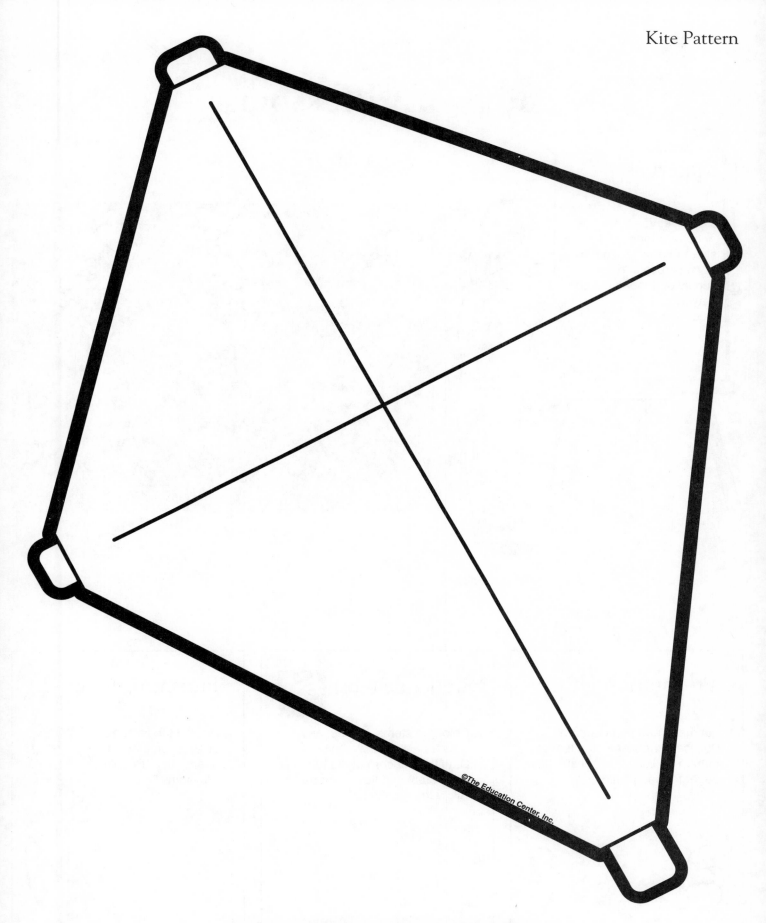

©The Education Center, Inc.

Popcorn Blossoms

Materials:

(for one project)

stems, leaves, and grass
    pattern (page 67)
sheet of 9" x 12" light blue
    construction paper
supply of popped popcorn
crayons
glue

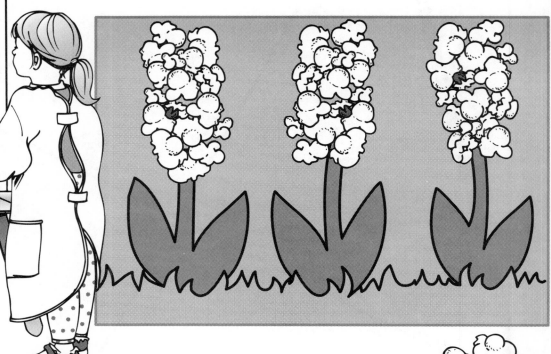

Preparation Hints:

1. Purchase and pop popcorn.
2. Duplicate the stems and leaves
    pattern on light blue construction
    paper for each child.

Student Steps:

1. Color the stems, leaves, and
    grass.
2. Glue the popcorn at the top of
    each stem in a flower shape.
3. Allow the glue to dry.

Finishing Touches:

1. Display the finished
    projects on a bulletin
    board titled "Poppin'
    Blossoms."

Lovely Ladybug

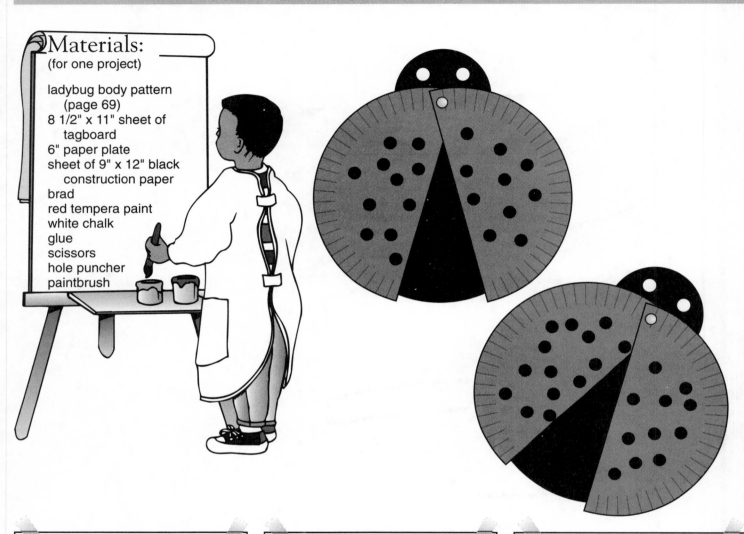

Materials:
(for one project)

ladybug body pattern
    (page 69)
8 1/2" x 11" sheet of
    tagboard
6" paper plate
sheet of 9" x 12" black
    construction paper
brad
red tempera paint
white chalk
glue
scissors
hole puncher
paintbrush

Preparation Hints:

1. Purchase paper plates and brads.
2. Duplicate the ladybug body pattern on tagboard and cut it out to use as a template.

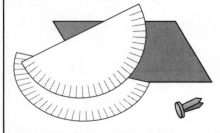

Student Steps:

Session 1:
1. Using the white chalk, trace a ladybug template on black construction paper.
2. Cut out the body and save the scraps.
3. Paint the paper plate red and allow to dry.

Session 2:
1. Fold the paper plate in half; then cut on the fold to make wings.
2. Use the brad to attach the wings to the body as shown.

3. Punch black dots from the scraps and glue to the wings.
4. Draw eyes on the ladybug with white chalk.

Finishing Touches:

1. Display the finished ladybugs with the poem "Ladybug, Ladybug, Fly Away Home."
2. Or display the ladybugs as a border for a spring bulletin board.

Adapted from an idea by Anne M. Cromwell-Gapp, Gr. Pre-K, Keene Day Care Center, Keene, NH

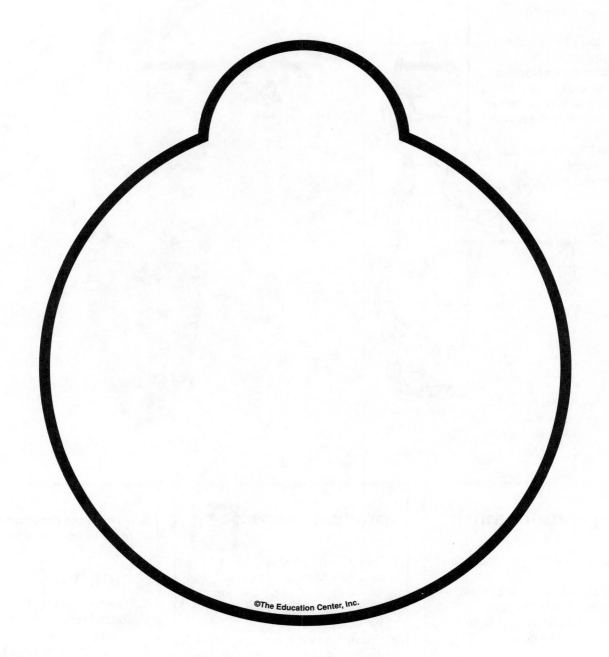

©The Education Center, Inc.

SPRING

Wiggle-Eye Butterfly

Materials:

(for one project)

butterfly body pattern
    (page 71)
tissue paper (various
    colors)
sheet of 9" x 12" brown
    construction paper
2 wiggle eyes
two 2" pieces of pipe
    cleaner
colored marker
glue
scissors

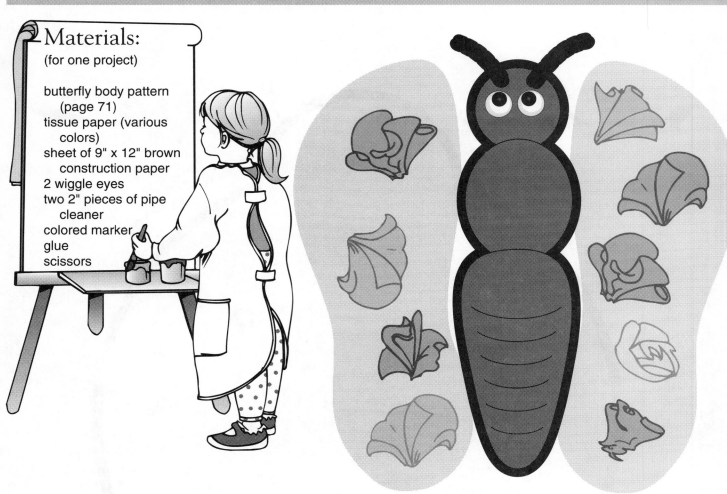

Preparation Hints:

1. Purchase wiggle eyes and pipe cleaners.
2. Cut pipe cleaners into pieces.
3. Duplicate a butterfly body pattern on brown construction paper for each child.

Student Steps:

1. Take off one shoe and trace around it twice on a sheet of tissue paper. Cut out the two outlines for butterfly wings. Save the scraps.
2. Crumple several small pieces of scrap tissue paper and glue them on the wings. Use scraps of tissue from classmates to get different colors.
3. Cut out the butterfly body pattern.
4. Glue on two wiggle eyes and two pipe-cleaner antennae.

5. Glue a wing to each side of the butterfly body as shown.

Finishing Touches:

1. Display the butterflies as a colorful spring border for a favorite bulletin board.
2. Or use the butterflies to decorate a reading corner while you read *The Very Hungry Caterpillar* by Eric Carle.

*Anne M. Cromwell-Gapp,
Gr. Pre-K, Keene Day Care Center,
Keene, NH*

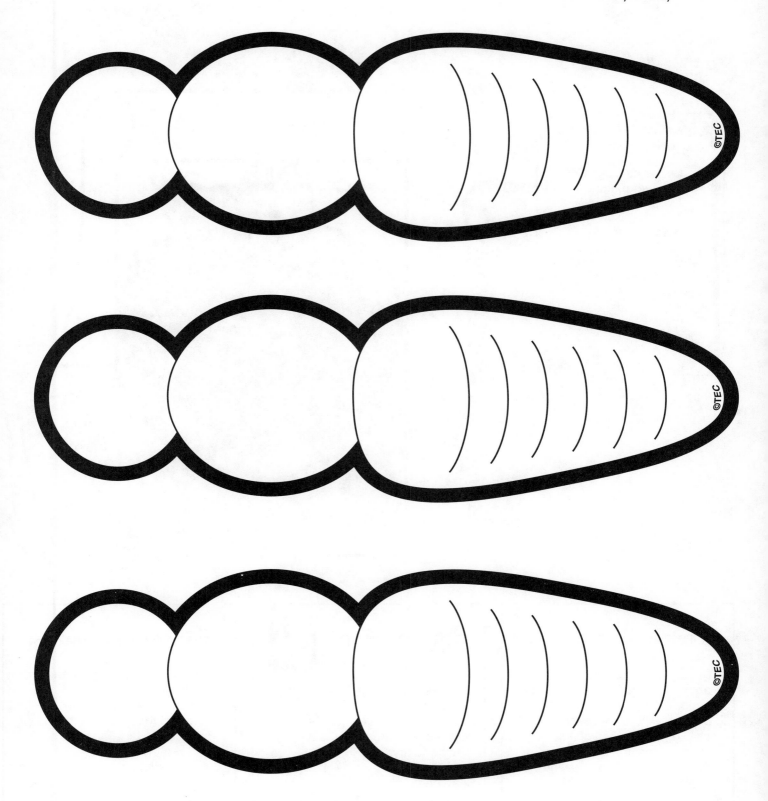

SPRING

Seed Story

Materials:
(for one project)

fruit patterns (pages 73–74)
book cover pattern
   (page 74)
sheets of 9" x 12" yellow,
   orange, and red
   construction paper
sheet of 9" x 12" colored
   construction paper
lemon, pumpkin, and
   apple seeds
crayons
glue
scissors
stapler

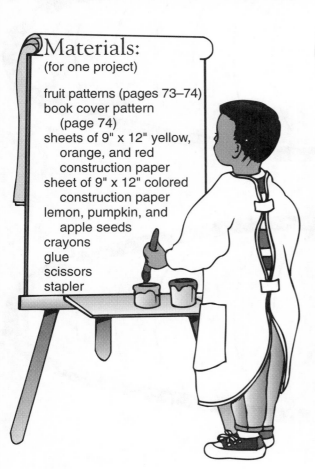

Preparation Hints:

1. Duplicate the fruit patterns on the appropriate colors of construction paper.
2. Duplicate the book cover for each child on the top half of a colored sheet of construction paper. Cut the sheet in half and use the bottom half as a back cover.
3. Collect fruit seeds.

Student Steps:

Session 1:
1. Cut out the fruit patterns on the heavy lines.
2. Glue the fruit seeds on the appropriate fruit cutouts and allow to dry.

Session 2:
1. Color the book cover.
2. Stack the cutouts between the front cover and back cover. Staple at the top edge.

Finishing Touches:

1. Help children write their names on the book covers.
2. Send the books home for students to share with their families.

*Beth Schimmel—Gr. Pre-K,
Blue Ridge Elementary,
Pinetop, AZ*

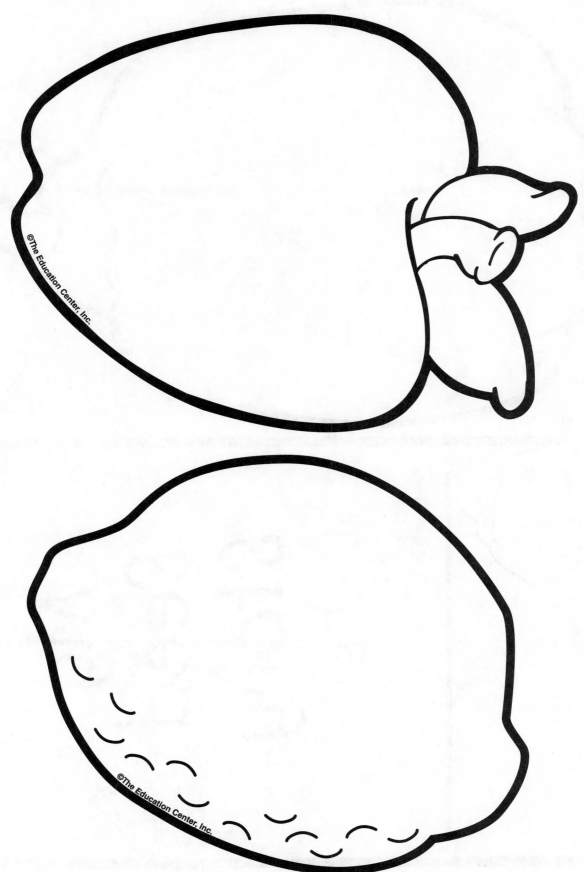

©The Education Center, Inc.

©The Education Center, Inc.

SPRING

Fruit Pattern

©The Education Center, Inc.

Book Cover Pattern

©The Education Center, Inc.

My
Seed
Story
by

Create A Bug

Materials:
(for one project)

two 6" colored construction-
  paper circles
5" colored construction-
  paper circle
1/2 sheet of 9" x 12" black
  construction paper
2 wing shapes (cut from
  laminating film)
crayons
scissors
stapler
glue

Preparation Hints:

1. Cut circles from colored construction paper.
2. Cut black construction paper into half sheets.
3. Cut excess laminating film into oval wing shapes (each about ten inches long).

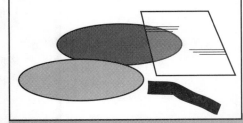

Student Steps:

1. Slightly overlap the two larger circles and glue them together.
2. Glue the smaller circle to one of the larger ones.
3. Cut six rectangles from black construction paper for legs and glue them on as shown.
4. Cut two antennae from black construction paper and glue to the bug's head.
5. Staple the wings to the center circle as shown.
6. Color facial features and any other desired markings.

Finishing Touches:

1. Help children identify the head, thorax, and abdomen of the insect.
2. Display the finished projects on a bulletin board titled "Buzz-A-Round Bugs."

Jayne M. Gammons—Grs. K & 1,
Oak Grove School,
Durham, NC

SPRING

Fuzzy Wuzzy Worm

Materials:
(for one project)

pom-poms (various sizes and colors)
2 wiggle eyes
1 1/2" piece of magnetic tape
glue

(back view)

*Jennifer Fry,
Kyrene School District,
Chandler, AZ*

Preparation Hints:

1. Purchase pom-poms, wiggle eyes, and magnetic tape.
2. Cut the magnetic tape into pieces.

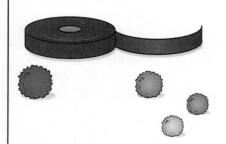

Student Steps:

Session 1:
1. Glue the desired sizes and colors of pom-poms together end to end to create a worm.
2. Glue two wiggle eyes to the worm's head.
3. Allow the glue to dry.

Session 2:
1. Attach a strip of magnetic tape to each worm.

Finishing Touches:

1. Have each child use his magnetic worm to attach good work to the refrigerator.

Ladybug Paperweight

Materials:
(for one project)

smooth, rounded rock
red tempera paint
1/2 of a black pipe
     cleaner
black permanent marker
craft glue
paintbrush

Preparation Hints:

1. Purchase rounded landscape rocks, pipe cleaners, and craft glue. (Craft glue is thicker and tackier than school glue.)
2. Wash and dry the rocks.
3. Cut the pipe cleaners into halves.

Student Steps:

Session 1:
1. Paint the rock with red tempera and allow to dry.

Session 2:
1. Use the black marker to draw the ladybug's eyes, dots, and wings.
2. Bend the pipe cleaner into a "U" shape and glue it to the ladybug's head as shown.

Finishing Touches:

1. Have students present the finished paperweights to family members as gifts.
2. Present the paperweights to the office staff on "Secretary's Day."

Adapted from an idea by Toni Petraglia—Gr. Pre-K, Reach Board Of Social Services, Somerville, NJ

SPRING

"Eggs-ceptional" Snail

Materials:
(for one project)

2-segment piece of
 cardboard egg carton
single segment of
 cardboard egg carton
3" piece of pipe cleaner
1" piece of pipe cleaner
2 wiggle eyes
tempera paint
craft glue
paintbrush

Preparation Hints:

1. Purchase pipe cleaners and wiggle eyes.
2. Collect and cut apart egg cartons.
3. Cut pipe cleaners into pieces.

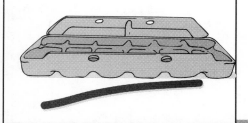

Student Steps:

Session 1:
1. Paint the egg carton segments and allow to dry.

Session 2:
1. Glue the single segment on top of the two-segment piece as shown.
2. Glue on wiggle eyes.
3. Bend the three-inch piece of pipe cleaner in the center and glue it to the snail's head for antennae.
4. Glue the one-inch piece of pipe cleaner to the back of the snail for a tail.

Finishing Touches:

1. Decorate your reading area with the finished snails, and then share the book, *The Snail's Spell,* by Joanne Ryder.

Cool Watermelon Slices

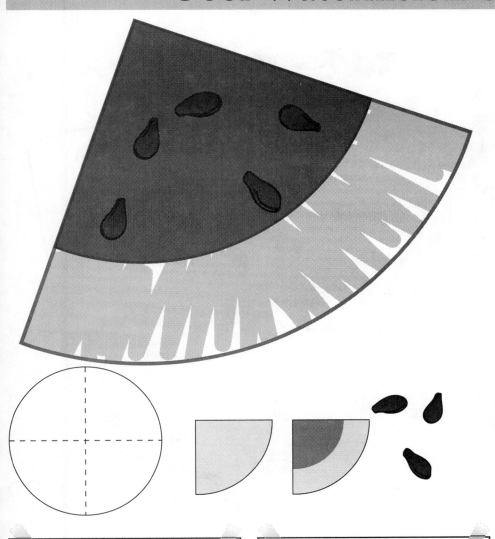

Materials:
(for one project)

1/4 of an 8" tagboard circle
1/4 of a 6" red tissue-
   paper circle
5 to 10 watermelon seeds
light green marker
glue

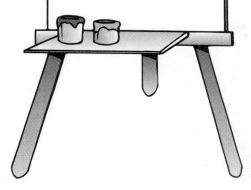

Preparation Hints:

1. Serve watermelon and have children save the seeds, or purchase the needed amount.
2. Cut out tagboard and tissue-paper circles; then cut each into fourths.

Student Steps:

1. Color the tagboard with a light green marker.
2. Glue the red tissue-paper pieces to the tagboard pieces as shown.
3. Glue watermelon seeds to the tissue-paper pieces and allow to dry.

Finishing Touches:

1. Display the watermelon slices around the edge of a bulletin board for a refreshing border.

Anne M. Cromwell-Gapp,
Gr. Pre-K,
Keene Day Care Center,
Keene, NH

SUMMER

Flashy Flag

Materials:

(for one project)

flag pattern (page 81)
sheet of 9" x 12" white
   construction paper
1" x 12" strip of a brown
   paper bag
red, white, and blue
   tempera paint
three 8" pieces of string
3 craft sticks
glue
tape
scissors
newspaper

Preparation Hints:

1. Duplicate the flag pattern on white construction paper for each child.
2. Collect paper bags and cut them into strips.
3. Collect newspaper.
4. Place each color of paint in a separate bowl.
5. Cut string into eight-inch pieces.

Student Steps:

Session 1:
1. Cover the work area with newspaper.
2. Cut out the flag pattern.
3. Tape a piece of string to the end of each craft stick.
4. Hold the craft stick and dip the string into one color of paint.
5. Drag the string across the flag pattern a few times.
6. Continue in this manner with all three colors of paint, and then allow to dry.

Session 2:
1. Glue a brown paper strip to the back for a flagpole.

Finishing Touches:

1. Display the flags in classroom windows for patriotic holidays.

Anne M. Cromwell-Gapp,
Gr. Pre-K,
Keene Day Care Center,
Keene, NH

©The Education Center, Inc.

SUMMER

Festive Fireworks

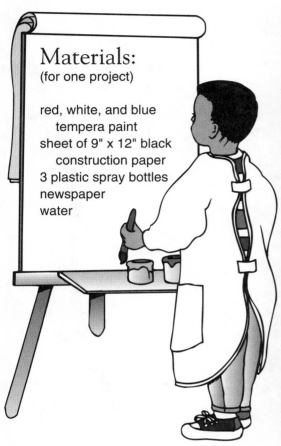

Materials:
(for one project)

red, white, and blue
    tempera paint
sheet of 9" x 12" black
    construction paper
3 plastic spray bottles
newspaper
water

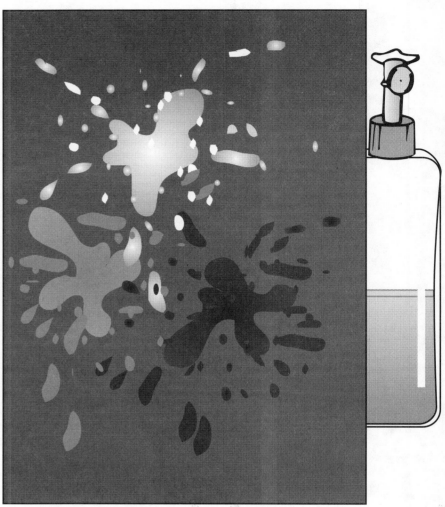

Preparation Hints:

1. Collect spray bottles and
   newspaper.
2. Slightly dilute each color of paint
   and place in a spray bottle.

Student Steps:

1. Cover your work surface with
   newspaper.
2. Place the black construction
   paper on top of the newspaper.
3. Spray each color of paint on the
   paper.

Finishing Touches:

1. Display these festive Fourth Of
   July paintings on a bulletin
   board titled "Happy Red, White,
   And Blue!"

Anne M. Cromwell-Gapp,
Gr. Pre-K, Keene Day Care Center,
Keene, NH

Star-Spangled Glasses

Materials:
(for one project)

pattern below
sheet of 9" x 12"
    construction paper (red,
    white, or blue)
two 12" lengths of yarn
glitter (red, blue, and silver)
ribbon (red, white, and blue)
star stickers
glue
scissors
hole puncher

Preparation Hints:

1. Gather the glitter, ribbon, and stickers.
2. Duplicate the glasses pattern on construction paper for each child.
3. Punch a hole through the lens portion of the patterns as a starting point for cutting. (Or, if desired, cut out the lens portion for younger students.)
4. Cut yarn into lengths and ribbon into pieces.

Student Steps:

1. Cut out the glasses pattern.
2. Cut out the lens portion of the glasses.
3. Punch holes in the outer corners as indicated.
4. Thread a length of yarn through each hole and knot to secure.
5. Glue on various colors of glitter.
6. Add ribbon pieces and star stickers.

Finishing Touches:

1. Have the children wear their glasses while marching to a patriotic song.

SUMMER

Beach In A Jar

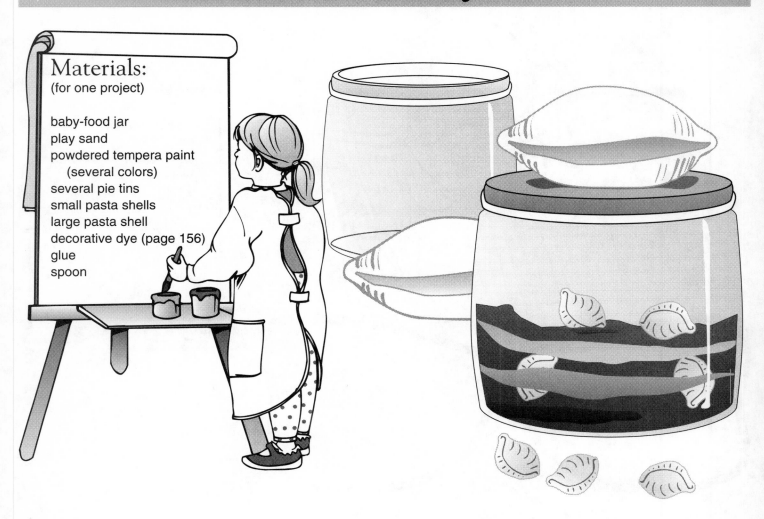

Materials:
(for one project)

baby-food jar
play sand
powdered tempera paint
   (several colors)
several pie tins
small pasta shells
large pasta shell
decorative dye (page 156)
glue
spoon

Preparation Hints:

1. Provide pasta shells and sand.
2. Collect baby-food jars, pie tins, and spoons.
3. Color the pasta shells using decorative dye and allow to dry.
4. Partially fill a baby-food jar with sand and add one teaspoon of tempera paint. Shake well to mix the color. Repeat with other colors in separate baby-food jars.
5. Pour each color of sand into a pie tin.

Student Steps:

1. Spoon layers of colored sand into the baby-food jar.
2. Add small pasta shells throughout the layers.
3. When the jar is completely full, glue the lid in place.
4. Glue the large pasta shell to the lid.

Finishing Touches:

1. Display the finished projects in a reading corner with books about the beach, such as *Katie And Kit At The Beach* by Tomie De Paola or *Beach Days* by Ken Robbins.

Carol A. Jasinski—Gr. Pre-K,
Buffalo Hearing And Speech
Center,
Buffalo, NY

Big Beach Ball

Materials:
(for one project)

two 12" circles of bulletin-
  board paper
tempera paint (various
  colors)
3 sheets of newspaper
12" length of yarn
paintbrush
stapler

Preparation Hints:

1. Collect newspaper.
2. Cut 12-inch circles from bulletin-
   board paper.
3. Cut yarn into 12-inch lengths.

Student Steps:

Session 1:
1. Paint designs on the large circles
   of paper and allow to dry.

Session 2:
1. Place the two circles together
   (decorated sides out) and staple
   the outer edges. Leave a six- to
   eight-inch opening.
2. Stuff the ball with crumpled
   newspaper.
3. Staple the opening closed.
4. Staple a length of yarn to the top.

Finishing Touches:

1. Suspend the beach balls from
   the ceiling over a table
   displaying books about the
   beach.

SUMMER

Necktie Notes

Materials:
(for one project)

necktie pattern (page 87)
sheet of 8 1/2" x 11"
    tagboard
tempera paint
3" x 4" white paper
    rectangles
marker
glue
scissors
paintbrush
stapler

Happy
Father's
Day

Preparation Hints:

1. Duplicate the necktie pattern on tagboard for each child.
2. Cut the white paper into 3" x 4" rectangles.

Student Steps:

Session 1:
1. Cut out the necktie pattern.
2. Paint the necktie and allow it to dry.

Session 2:
1. Make a notepad by stapling together several paper rectangles.
2. Glue the back page of the notepad to the tie as shown.
3. Write a special message on the first sheet of the notepad.

Finishing Touches:

1. Have children present the notepads as birthday or special occasion gifts.

Anne M. Cromwell-Gapp,
Gr. Pre-K, Keene Day Care Center,
Keene, NH

Necktie Pattern

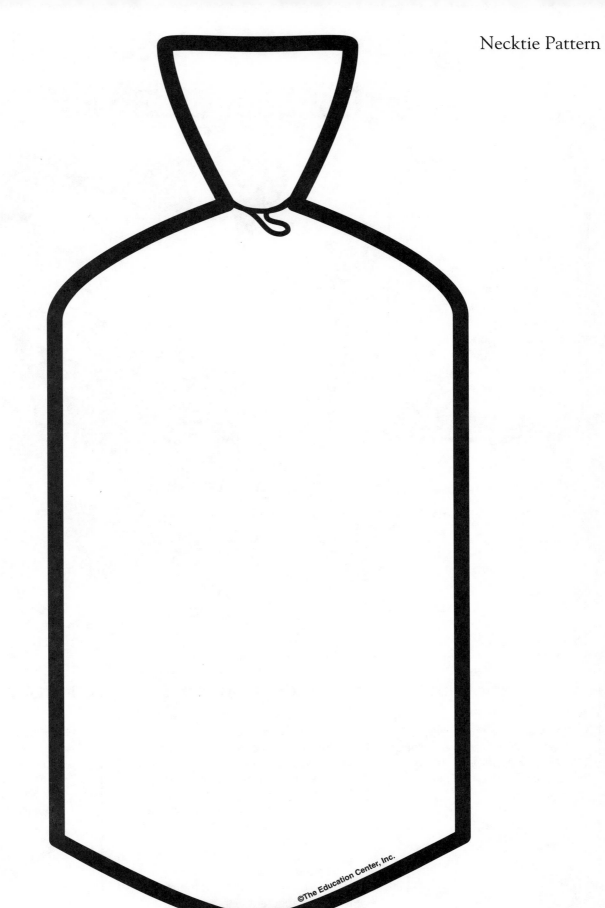

©The Education Center, Inc.

©1995 The Education Center, Inc. • *Arts And Crafts For Little Hands* • TEC891

87

GIFTS

A Bouquet Of Roses

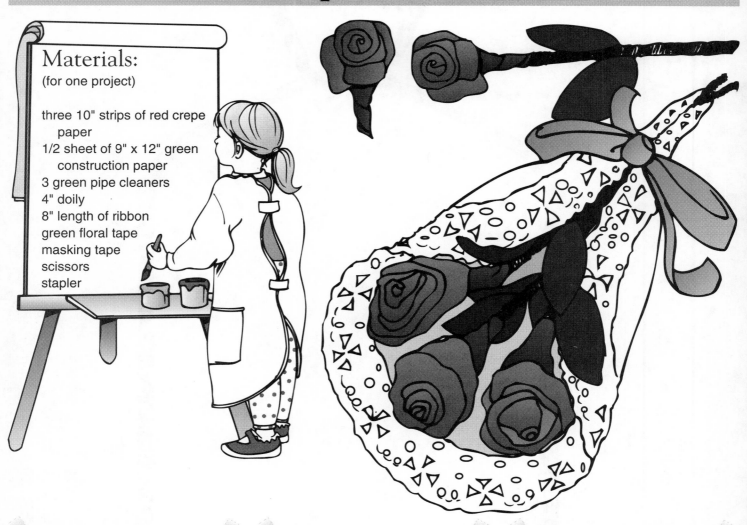

Materials:

(for one project)

three 10" strips of red crepe
  paper
1/2 sheet of 9" x 12" green
  construction paper
3 green pipe cleaners
4" doily
8" length of ribbon
green floral tape
masking tape
scissors
stapler

Preparation Hints:

1. Purchase crepe paper, pipe
   cleaners, floral tape, and doilies.
2. Cut crepe paper into strips.
3. Cut ribbon into eight-inch
   lengths.

Student Steps:

1. Loosely roll a strip of crepe paper
   into a rose and tape the end with
   masking tape.
2. Use floral tape to attach the rose
   to the top of a pipe cleaner.
3. Cut out green construction-paper
   leaves and tape them to the pipe
   cleaner.
4. Repeat Steps 1–3 to make two
   more roses.
5. Fold the doily around the roses
   and secure it with a staple.
6. Tie a length of ribbon around the
   bouquet.

Finishing Touches:

1. Have children present the
   bouquets to their mothers or
   special school volunteers.

*Judy Massengale—Gr. K,
Eastside Elementary School,
Senoia, GA*

Rainbow Rock

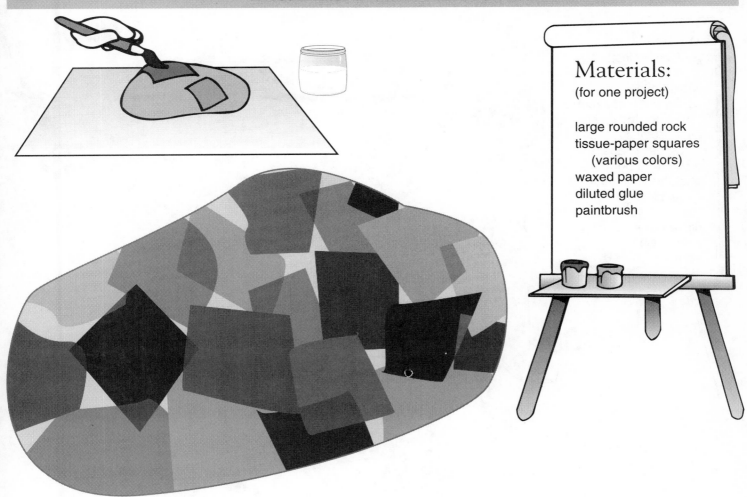

Materials:
(for one project)

large rounded rock
tissue-paper squares
 (various colors)
waxed paper
diluted glue
paintbrush

Preparation Hints:

1. Purchase smooth, round landscape rocks.
2. Wash and dry the rocks.
3. Cut the tissue paper into squares.

Student Steps:

1. Spread a sheet of waxed paper on top of the work surface.
2. Lay a square of tissue paper on the rock and paint over it with the diluted glue as shown.
3. Continue painting over squares until the rock is completely covered.
4. Allow the glue to dry.

Finishing Touches:

1. Have each child wrap his rainbow-rock paperweight in a piece of student-made wrapping paper and give to a family member as a gift.

GIFTS

Patchwork Portrait

Materials:

(for one project)

waxed paper
cardboard frame (cut to
   the desired size)
fabric scraps (cut in
   various shapes)
magnetic tape
photograph (student
   supplied)
masking tape
diluted glue
paintbrush
scissors

Preparation Hints:

1. Cut magnetic tape into small pieces.
2. Have students bring in photographs (school portraits).
3. Collect cardboard and cut into frames to fit the photos.
4. Collect and cut fabric scraps into shapes.

Student Steps:

Session 1:
1. Cover the work surface with waxed paper and lay down the frame.
2. Brush diluted glue onto both sides of a fabric piece, and then press onto the frame.
3. Continue overlapping fabric pieces until the cardboard is covered.
4. Allow the frame to dry. (If necessary, place the dried frame under a heavy book to flatten it.)

Session 2:
1. Cut off the excess fabric around the edge of the frame.
2. Attach magnetic tape pieces to the back of the frame.
3. Attach the photo to the back of the frame with masking tape.

Finishing Touches:

1. Have children present the framed photos to parents or grandparents for birthdays or other special occasions.
2. Display each frame on the family refrigerator.

Snappy Sun Visor

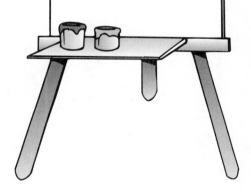

Materials:
(for one project)

plastic sun visor
fabric paint in squeeze
    bottles (various colors)
newspaper

Preparation Hints:

1. Purchase fabric paint and plastic sun visors at a craft store.
2. Collect newspaper.

Student Steps:

1. Spread newspaper on top of the work surface.
2. Use the fabric paint to decorate the sun visor with squiggles, lines, dots, or designs.
3. Allow the paint to dry.

Finishing Touches:

1. Children can give the sun visors as gifts to family members or take them home for summer vacation.

*Suzanne Costner,
Maryville, TN*

GIFTS

Super Sun Catcher

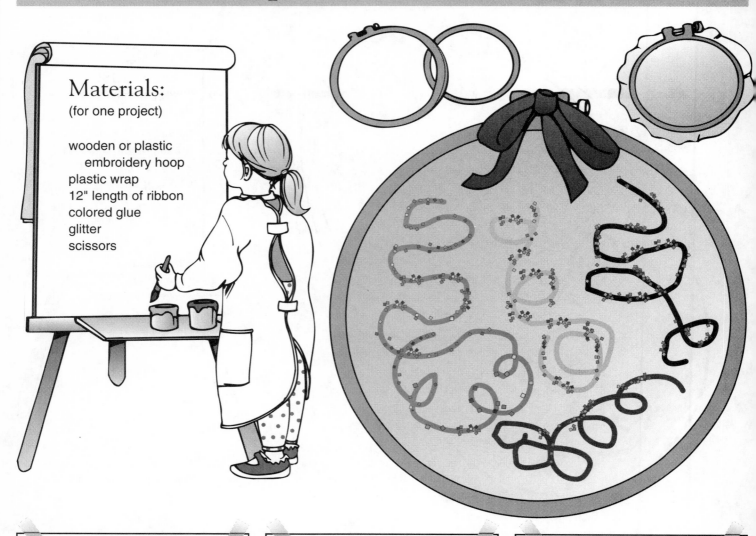

Materials:
(for one project)

wooden or plastic
 embroidery hoop
plastic wrap
12" length of ribbon
colored glue
glitter
scissors

Preparation Hints:

1. Provide hoops, plastic wrap, ribbon, colored glue, and glitter.
2. Cut plastic wrap into hoop-sized squares.
3. Cut ribbon into lengths.

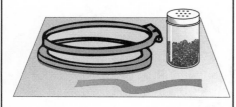

Student Steps:

1. Secure a piece of plastic wrap between the two hoop segments.
2. Cut off the excess plastic wrap from around the hoop.
3. Tie a length of ribbon on the clasp of the hoop.
4. Squeeze trails of colored glue on top of the plastic wrap and sprinkle with glitter.
5. Shake off the excess glitter and allow the glue to dry.

Finishing Touches:

1. Have children present the finished projects to hospital patients or residents of a nursing home.
2. Display the sun catchers in classroom windows for decoration.

Mary E. Maurer—Gr. pre-K, Caddo, OK

Jazzy Jewelry

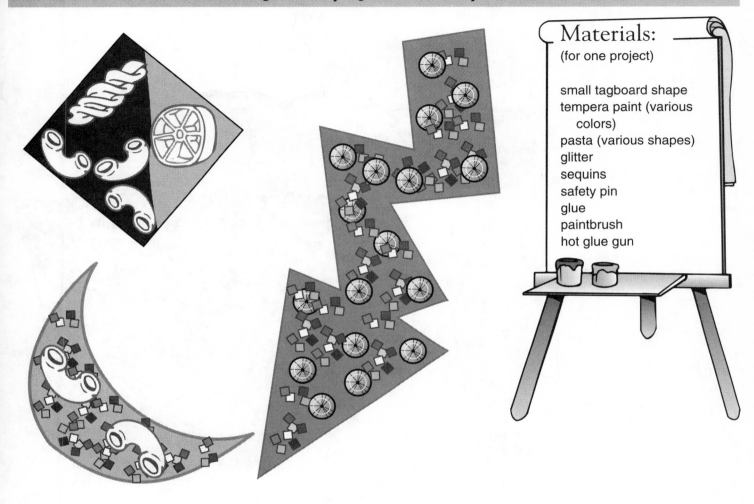

Materials:
(for one project)

small tagboard shape
tempera paint (various colors)
pasta (various shapes)
glitter
sequins
safety pin
glue
paintbrush
hot glue gun

Preparation Hints:

1. Gather pasta, glitter, sequins, and safety pins.
2. Cut tagboard into a variety of shapes (about two to three inches wide).

Student Steps:

Session 1:
1. Choose a tagboard shape.
2. Paint it on one side and allow to dry.

Session 2:
1. Glue pasta, glitter, and sequins on the painted side and allow the glue to dry.

Finishing Touches:

1. Using the hot glue gun, secure a safety pin to the back of the jewelry piece.
2. Have each child wrap his jewelry in tissue paper and present to someone special.

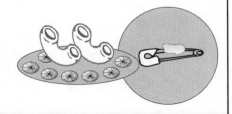

GIFTS

Cheery Candy Cup

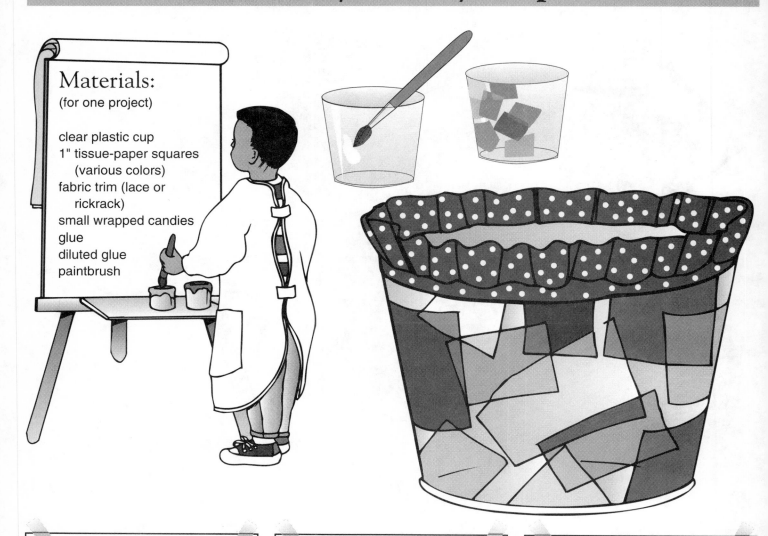

Materials:
(for one project)

clear plastic cup
1" tissue-paper squares
    (various colors)
fabric trim (lace or
    rickrack)
small wrapped candies
glue
diluted glue
paintbrush

Preparation Hints:

1. Gather clear cups, fabric trim, and candies.
2. Cut tissue paper into squares.
3. Dilute some white glue.

Student Steps:

1. Paint a coat of diluted glue on the outside of the cup.
2. Press on tissue-paper squares, overlapping them to cover the whole cup.
3. Glue a length of fabric trim around the open edge of the cup.
4. Allow the glue to dry.

Finishing Touches:

1. Fill the cups with candies and have students present them as gifts to cafeteria workers or custodial staff.

Handprint Hoop

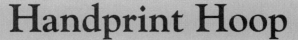

Materials:
(for one project)

12" wooden or plastic
    embroidery hoop
14" circle of muslin
red tempera paint
fabric paint in squeeze
    bottles (various colors)
5" length of ribbon
paintbrush
hot glue gun

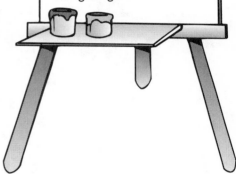

Preparation Hints:

1. Purchase hoops, muslin, ribbon, and fabric paints at a craft store.
2. Cut the muslin into 14-inch circles.
3. Cut the ribbon into lengths. Tie each length into a bow.

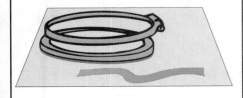

Student Steps:

Session 1:
1. Have an adult paint each of your hands with red paint.
2. Press your hands onto the muslin circle and allow the paint to dry.

Session 2:
1. Use a variety of fabric paints to decorate on and around the handprints with dots, squiggles, and zigzags.
2. Allow the paint to dry.

Finishing Touches:

1. Insert the muslin between the hoops and glue in place with hot glue.
2. Glue the bow to the top of the hoop with the hot glue gun.
3. Have the children present the hoops to parents or grandparents as mementos.

Adapted from an idea by Janet Keyser Carnes—Gr. K, K. W. Bergan School, Browning, MT

GIFTS

Autograph Mat

Materials:
(for one project)

alphabet sponges
12" x 18" sheet of
    construction paper
tempera paint (various
    colors)
disposable pie pans
clear adhesive vinyl
crayons or markers

Preparation Hints:

1. Purchase alphabet sponges and clear adhesive vinyl.
2. Collect disposable pie pans.
3. Pour one color of paint into each pie pan.

Student Steps:

Session 1:
1. Choose the alphabet sponges needed to spell your name.
2. Use the sponges to print your name on the construction paper in the colors desired.
3. Allow the paint to dry.

Session 2:
1. Decorate around your name with the crayons or markers.

Finishing Touches:

1. Cover the mats with clear adhesive vinyl (or laminate, if desired).
2. Use the mats all year long for painting and gluing activities.

Adapted from an idea by Brenda Hirchert—Gr. Pre-K, St. Luke's Child Care Village, Kearney, NE

Hum 'n' Toot Tube

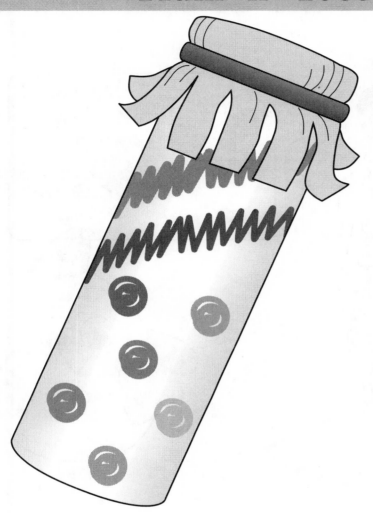

Materials:
(for one project)

paper-towel tube
4" tissue-paper circle
tempera paint (various
   colors)
rubber band
scissors
paintbrush
markers

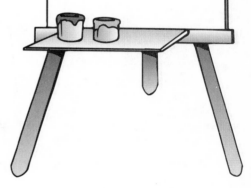

Preparation Hints:

1. Collect paper-towel tubes.
2. Cut circles from tissue paper.

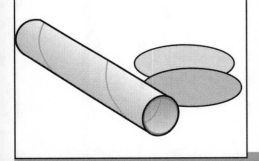

Student Steps:

Session 1:
1. Decorate the tube with paint or markers and allow to dry.

Session 2:
1. Cover one end of the tube with a tissue-paper circle and secure with a rubber band.
2. Fringe the loose tissue paper below the rubber band.
3. Make a humming noise in the open end of the tube.

Finishing Touches:

1. Have the children use the tubes for a musical parade.

ANYTIME

Soap Critter

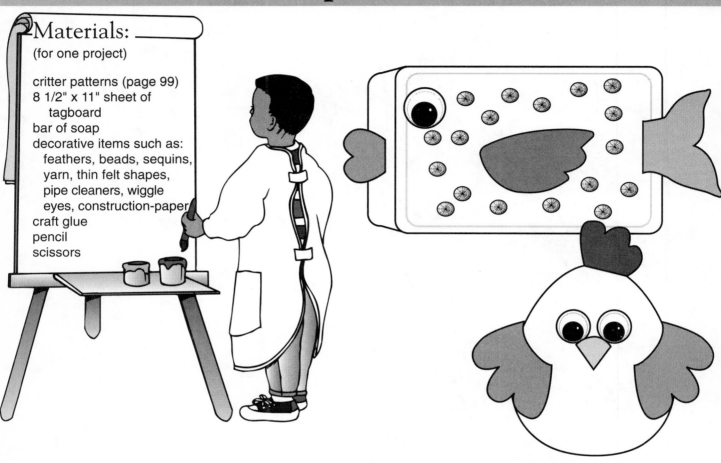

Materials:

(for one project)

critter patterns (page 99)
8 1/2" x 11" sheet of
 tagboard
bar of soap
decorative items such as:
 feathers, beads, sequins,
 yarn, thin felt shapes,
 pipe cleaners, wiggle
 eyes, construction-paper
craft glue
pencil
scissors

Preparation Hints:

1. Collect soap, decorative items, and craft glue. (Craft glue is thicker and tackier than school glue.)
2. Duplicate the critter patterns on tagboard and cut out to use as templates.

Student Steps:

1. Decide what type of critter to make: bunny, chick, mouse, or fish.
2. Use the templates to trace and cut out patterns, if desired.
3. Glue features to the soap using the cutouts and decorative items.

Finishing Touches:

1. Allow the glue to dry and display the finished critters on a table labeled "Crafty Critters."

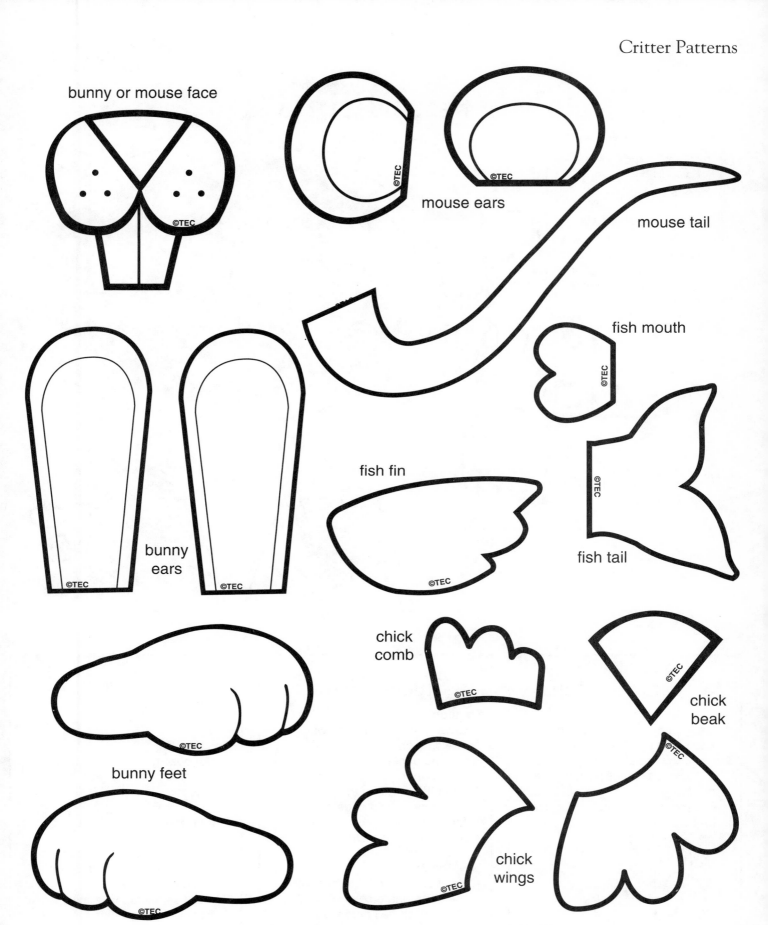

bunny or mouse face

mouse ears

mouse tail

fish mouth

bunny ears

fish fin

fish tail

chick comb

chick beak

bunny feet

chick wings

ANYTIME

Pizza Prints

Materials:

(for one project)

12" circle of manila paper
tempera paint (red, brown, green, and white)
fresh mushroom, pepper, and onion (each cut in half)
short pieces of yellow yarn
newspaper
glue
paintbrush

Preparation Hints:

1. Gather peppers, mushrooms, and onions.
2. Cut the vegetables in half.
3. Cut 12-inch circles from manila paper.
4. Cut yellow yarn into short pieces.
5. Collect newspaper.

Student Steps:

Session 1:
1. Cover the work surface with newspaper.
2. Lay the paper circle on top of the newspaper.
3. Paint the inside of the circle red, leaving a manila edge showing for crust.
4. Allow the paint to dry.

Session 2:
1. Paint each vegetable half with the appropriate color of paint. Press each half onto the pizza several times to represent toppings.
2. Allow the paint to dry.

Session 3:
1. Squeeze glue over the toppings. Sprinkle pieces of yarn on the glue for cheese.

Finishing Touches:

1. Display the finished projects on a bulletin board with the school lunch menu.
2. Have students make mini pizzas from English muffins for a snack.

Name Necklace

Materials:
(for one project)

salt dough (page 156)
tempera paint
24" length of yarn
cookie cutter (in a simple
   shape)
waxed paper
rolling pin
pencil
paintbrush

Preparation Hints:

1. Prepare salt dough.
2. Collect cookie cutters and rolling pin.
3. Cut yarn into lengths.

Student Steps:

Session 1:
1. Roll out salt dough on waxed paper to a thickness of about 1/4 inch.
2. Use the cookie cutter to cut out a shape from the dough.
3. Use a pencil to etch your name in the cutout shape and to make a hole at the top of the medallion.
4. Allow the shape to harden for about two days.

Session 2:
1. Paint the hardened medallion with tempera and allow to dry.

Session 3:
1. Thread the yarn through the hole and tie the ends.

Finishing Touches:

1. Children can wear their necklaces as nametags when a substitute teacher is working in the classroom.

ANYTIME

Stitch-A-Lei

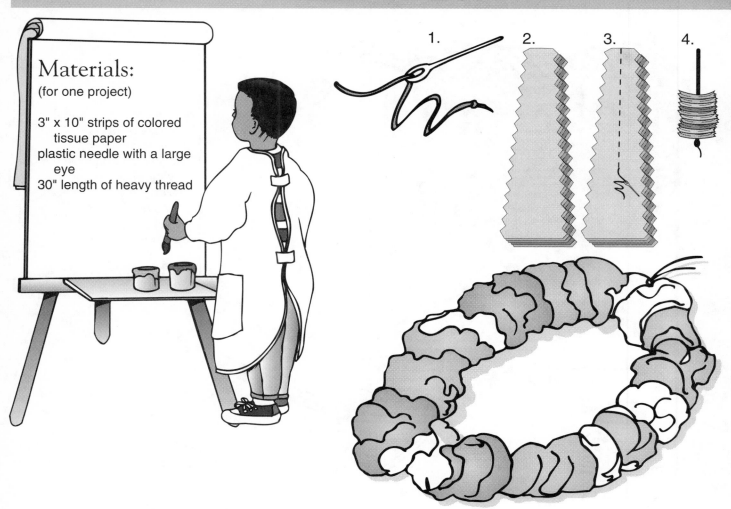

Materials:
(for one project)

3" x 10" strips of colored
   tissue paper
plastic needle with a large
   eye
30" length of heavy thread

1. 2. 3. 4.

Preparation Hints:

1. Use pinking shears to cut strips
   of colored tissue paper.
2. Purchase plastic needles (such
   as yarn needles) at a craft store.
3. Cut heavy thread into lengths.

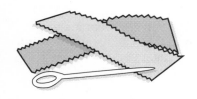

Student Steps:

1. Thread the needle and tie a knot
   at one end of the thread (see the
   illustration for Step 1).
2. Stack together two strips of
   tissue paper.
3. Make a running stitch down the
   center of the tissue paper at
   about one-inch intervals (see the
   illustration for Step 3).
4. Gather the tissue paper toward
   the knot (see the illustration for
   Step 4).
5. Sew and gather more double

strips of tissue paper until the
   thread is about half covered.
6. Tie the ends of the thread
   together in a knot.
7. Gently separate the layers of
   tissue paper to create a fluffy
   look.

Finishing Touches:

1. Have the children wear their leis
   while listening to you read the
   book *A Is For Aloha* by
   Stephanie Feeney.

"Bubble-rific" Card

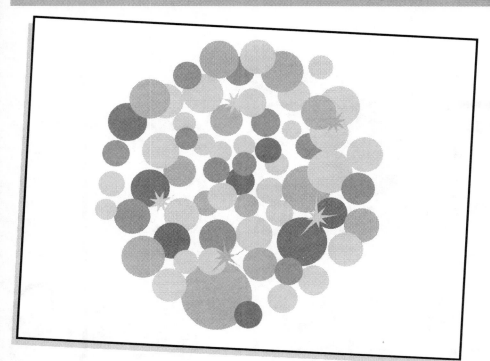

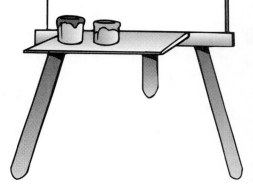

Materials:
(for one project)

sheet of 9" x 12" white
  construction paper
several bowls of water
tempera paint (various
  colors)
plastic straws

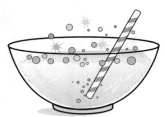

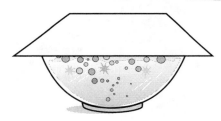

Preparation Hints:

1. Have the children bring in plastic straws.
2. Mix approximately one tablespoon of tempera paint with 1/4 cup of water in each bowl.

Student Steps:

1. Place a straw into one bowl of paint water and blow to create bubbles. Be careful not to suck the water up through the straw!
2. Immediately place the construction paper on top of the bubbles.
3. Repeat Steps 1 and 2 using other paint colors.

Finishing Touches:

1. Display the finished paintings on a bulletin board titled "Bubble Bursts."
2. Have the children fold their papers painted sides out and use them as greeting cards or thank-you notes for special occasions.

ANYTIME

Topsy-Turvy Clown

Materials:
(for one project)

clown patterns (page 105)
sheet of 9" x 12" colored
    construction paper
brad
decorative materials such
    as: glitter, sequins,
    beads, rickrack
crayons or markers
scissors
glue

Preparation Hints:

1. Provide brads and decorative materials.
2. Duplicate the clown patterns on colored construction paper for each child.

Student Steps:

1. Cut out the clown patterns.
2. Push the brad through the dots to connect the two pieces.
3. Color the clown's facial features.
4. Glue decorative materials to the clown's clothes.

Finishing Touches:

1. Have a parade of twisting and turning clowns while marching to circus music.
2. Display the clowns as a colorful border around a circus-theme bulletin board.

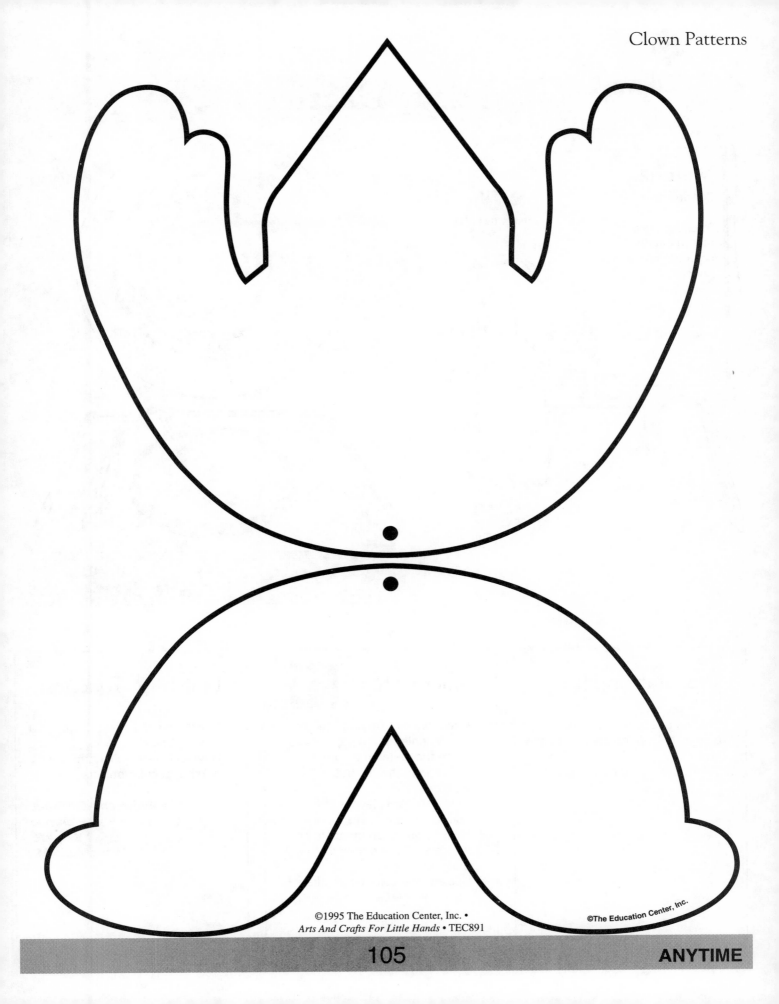

Clown Patterns

©1995 The Education Center, Inc. •
Arts And Crafts For Little Hands • TEC891

©The Education Center, Inc.

105

ANYTIME

Dizzy Dazzler

Materials:

(for one project)

9" paper plate
record player
colored markers
pencil

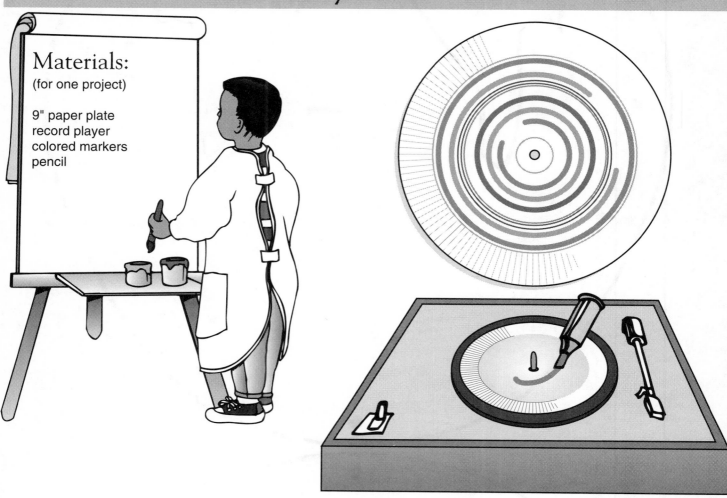

Preparation Hints:

1. Obtain paper plates and poke a small hole in the center of each one.
2. Set up the record player.

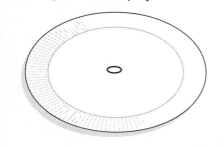

Student Steps:

1. Use a pencil to enlarge the hole in the center of the paper plate.
2. Place the plate on the record player (see the illustration above).
3. Set the record player at the 45 speed and turn it on.
4. Hold a marker on the plate and watch the design form as the plate spins.
5. Use several colors of markers to complete the design.

Finishing Touches:

1. Display the finished artwork on a bulletin board.
2. Have children brainstorm a list of other circular objects.

*Kathy Anderson—Gr. Pre-K,
Learn And Play Preschool
I.S.D. #16,
Minneapolis, MN*

Collage Creation

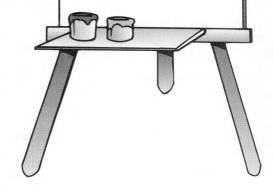

Materials:
(for one project)

9" x 12" cardboard rectangle
construction-paper scraps
  (various colors)
two 1 1/2" x 9" strips of
  black construction paper
two 1 1/2" x 12" strips of
  black construction paper
glue
scissors

Preparation Hints:

1. Collect cardboard rectangles. (The sides of cereal boxes work well.)
2. Cut black construction paper into strips.

Student Steps:

Session 1:
1. Cut a variety of shapes from the construction-paper scraps.
2. Glue the shapes to the cardboard, overlapping the edges to completely cover the rectangle. Allow the glue to dry.

Session 2:
1. To make a frame, glue construction-paper strips along the edges of the collage.

Finishing Touches:

1. Read some books by Ezra Jack Keats, such as *The Snowy Day* or *Whistle For Willie*, and discuss collage as an illustration technique.

Blow-A-Bubble

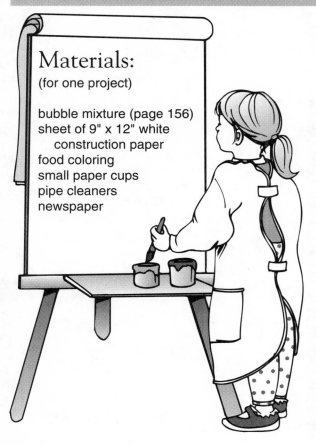

Materials:

(for one project)

bubble mixture (page 156)
sheet of 9" x 12" white
   construction paper
food coloring
small paper cups
pipe cleaners
newspaper

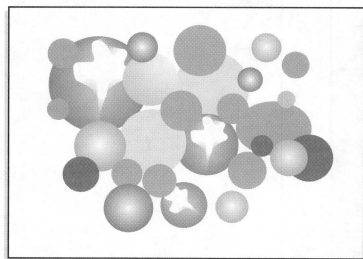

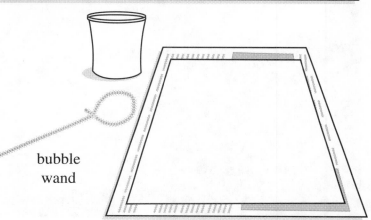

bubble
wand

Preparation Hints:

1. Prepare bubble mixture and divide into small paper cups.
2. Mix a different color of food coloring into each cup.

Student Steps:

1. To make bubble wands, bend the ends of pipe cleaners to form circles and twist to secure (see the illustration above).
2. Spread newspaper on top of the work surface.
3. Place the white construction paper on the newspaper.
4. Dip the bubble wand into a cup of bubble mixture and gently blow bubbles onto the paper.
5. Repeat Step 4 with other colors and bubble wands.

Finishing Touches:

1. As an outside variation, attach the white paper to a chain-link fence; then have the children blow bubbles and try to hit the paper.

Ann Scalley—Gr. Pre-K,
Wellfleet Preschool,
Wellfleet, MA

Puzzling Picture

Materials:
(for one project)

6 craft sticks
masking tape
colored markers

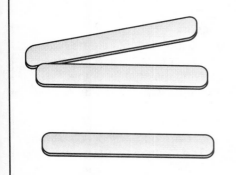

Preparation Hints:

1. Collect craft sticks.

Student Steps:

1. Place the craft sticks side by side.
2. Tape the sticks together with strips of masking tape (see the illustration above).
3. Turn the sticks over and color a design.
4. Remove the tape from the back.
5. Mix up the sticks and try to reassemble the picture.

Finishing Touches:

1. Bind each child's set of puzzle sticks with a rubber band and send home for some family fun.

*Debra Damiano,
Gr. K: Special Education,
Ash Street Center,
Forest Park, GA*

Shipshape Sailor Hat

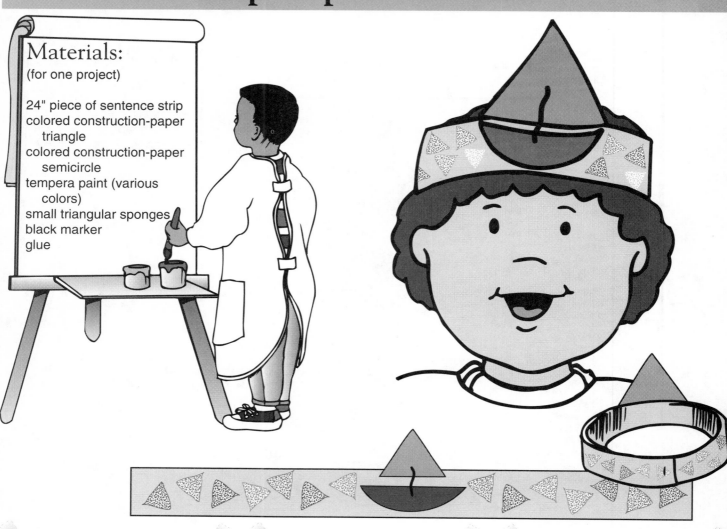

Materials:

(for one project)

24" piece of sentence strip
colored construction-paper
   triangle
colored construction-paper
   semicircle
tempera paint (various
   colors)
small triangular sponges
black marker
glue

Preparation Hints:

1. Cut sentence strip pieces.
2. Cut construction paper into two-inch squares; then cut the squares into triangles.
3. Cut construction paper into 2 1/2" x 1 1/2" pieces; then cut out semicircles.
4. Cut sponges into small triangular shapes.

Student Steps:

Session 1:
1. Glue the triangle and semicircle to the sentence strip as shown.
2. Draw a line connecting the two shapes.
3. Make triangle prints on the sentence strip using the sponges and paint.
4. Allow the paint to dry.

Session 2:
1. Staple the ends of the sentence strip together.

Finishing Touches:

1. Encourage the children to wear the headbands while singing "Row, Row, Row Your Boat" or "My Bonny Lies Over The Ocean."
2. Have the students create hats for other occasions or themes by varying the shapes of the cutouts (such as hearts for Valentine's Day).

Carmen Sortino—Gr. Pre-K, The College Of Staten Island's Children's Center, Staten Island, NY

Ping-Pong® Painting

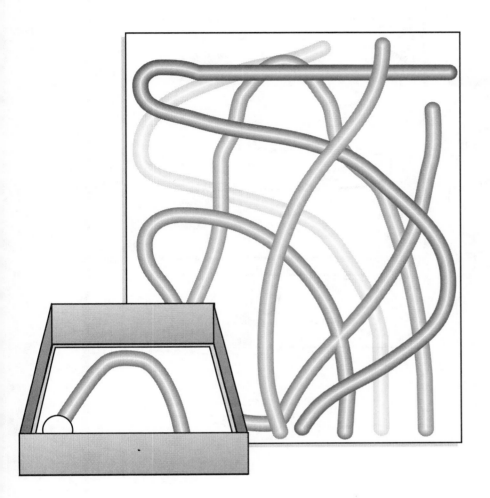

Materials:

(for one project)

sheet of 9" x 12"
   construction paper
box (large enough to lay
   the paper in the bottom)
several Ping-Pong balls
tempera paint (various
   colors)

Preparation Hints:

1. Collect boxes and Ping-Pong balls.

Student Steps:

1. Place the construction paper inside the box.
2. Dip a Ping-Pong ball in a color of paint and put it in the box.
3. Move the box around, rolling the ball and making a trail of paint.
4. Repeat Steps 2 and 3 with other colors of paint and allow to dry.

Finishing Touches:

1. Display the finished artwork on a bulletin board titled "Ping-Pong Roll-Along."
2. Have children try to trace the various paths in each picture.

Debra Damiano,
Gr. K: Special Education,
Ash Street Center,
Forest Park, GA

ANYTIME

Window Whale

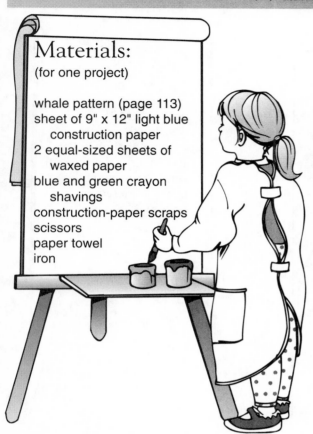

Materials:
(for one project)

whale pattern (page 113)
sheet of 9" x 12" light blue
   construction paper
2 equal-sized sheets of
   waxed paper
blue and green crayon
   shavings
construction-paper scraps
scissors
paper towel
iron

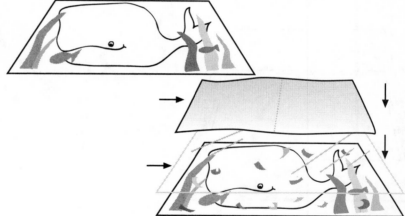

Preparation Hints:

1. Duplicate the whale pattern on light blue construction paper for each child.
2. Collect an iron and blue and green crayons.
3. Make blue and green crayon shavings using a pencil sharpener.

Student Steps:

1. Cut out the whale pattern and place it on top of one sheet of waxed paper.
2. Cut small ocean shapes (such as fish or plants) from the construction-paper scraps. Lay these on the waxed paper.
3. Sprinkle crayon shavings over the ocean scene.
4. Place the other sheet of waxed paper over the scene, aligning the edges.

Finishing Touches:

1. Place a paper towel on top of each child's waxed paper; then press with a warm iron to melt the crayon shavings and seal the sheets together.
2. Display the whale scenes in classroom windows during a unit of study on the ocean.

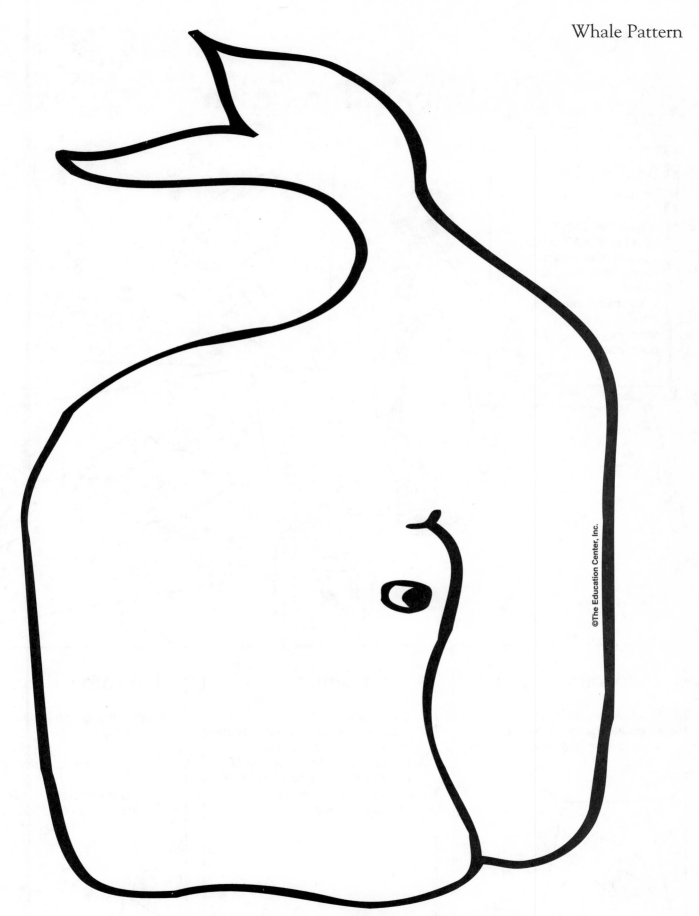

ANYTIME

Fabulous Fish

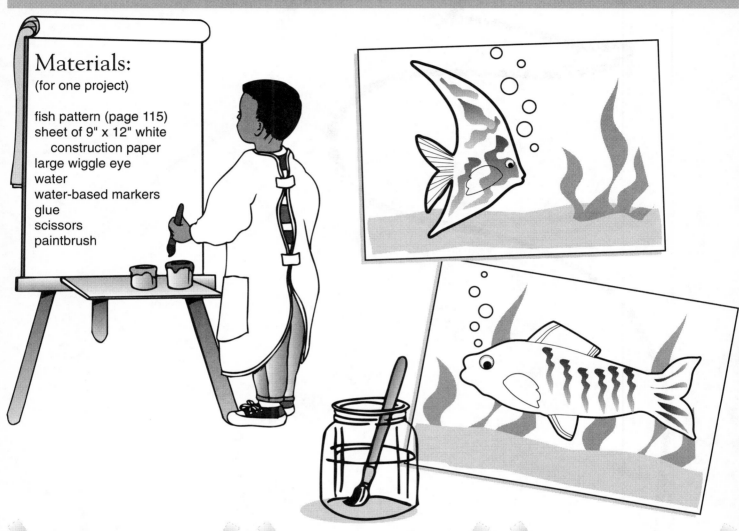

Materials:
(for one project)

fish pattern (page 115)
sheet of 9" x 12" white
   construction paper
large wiggle eye
water
water-based markers
glue
scissors
paintbrush

Preparation Hints:

1. Purchase wiggle eyes.
2. Duplicate the fish pattern on white construction paper for each child.

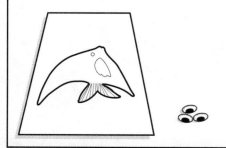

Student Steps:

1. Cut out the fish pattern.
2. Draw designs on the fish with the markers. Use several colors.
3. Dip the paintbrush in the water and brush it over the fish cutout.
4. Allow the fish to dry, and then glue on a wiggle eye.

Finishing Touches:

1. Display the fish on a classroom ocean mural.
2. Suspend the fish from the ceiling for a classroom aquarium effect.

Carmen Sortino—Gr. Pre-K,
The College Of Staten Island's
Children's Center,
Staten Island, NY

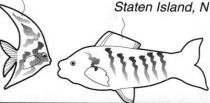

©The Education Center, Inc.

©The Education Center, Inc.

Squares To Go

Materials:

(for one project)

transportation patterns
(page 117)
8 1/2" x 11" sheet of
tagboard
1/2 sheet of large-square
graph paper
sheet of 9" x 12"
construction paper
crayons or markers
pencil
glue
scissors

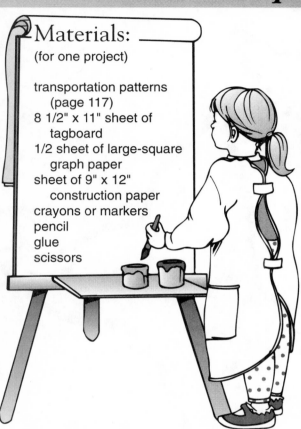

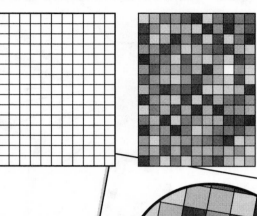

Preparation Hints:

1. Obtain large-square graph
paper and cut into half sheets.
2. Duplicate the transportation
patterns on tagboard and cut out
for use as templates.

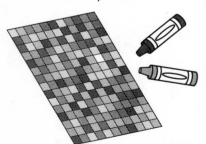

Student Steps:

1. Color each square on the graph
paper using different colors.
2. Choose a template and trace
the outline on the graph paper.
3. Cut out the outline.
4. Glue the cutout to the
construction paper.

Finishing Touches:

1. Display the finished projects on a
transportation-theme bulletin
board titled "Way To Go!"
2. Use the finished artwork on a
wall-size bar graph to have
students vote for their favorite
way to travel: air, land, or water.

Mary Langford—Gr. K,
St. Agnes School,
Butler, WI

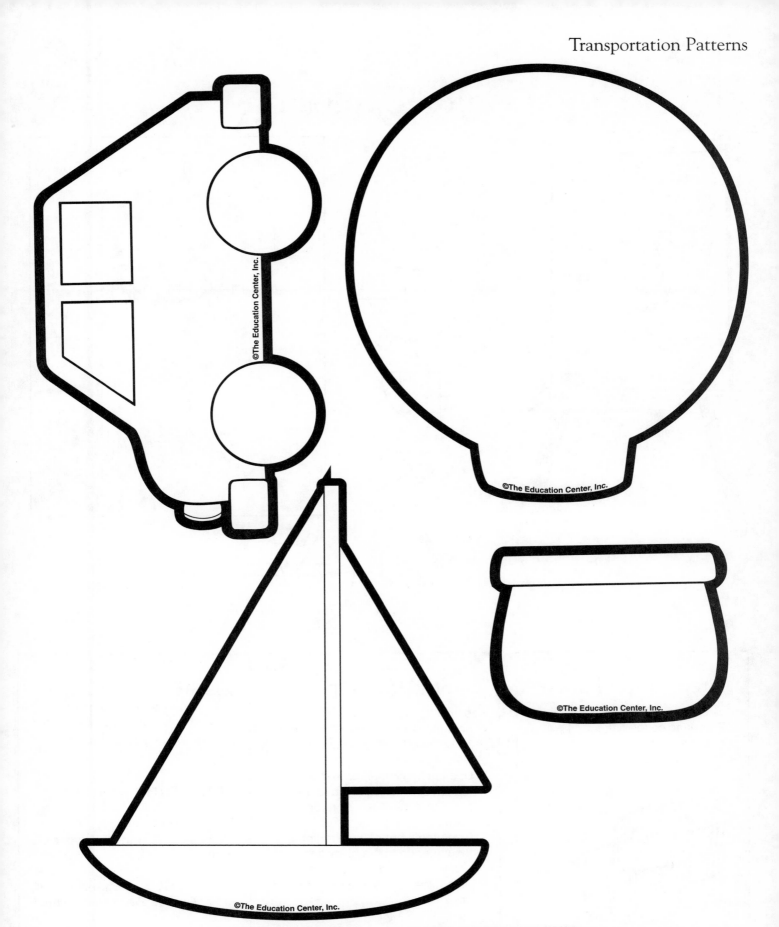

©The Education Center, Inc.

©The Education Center, Inc.

©The Education Center, Inc.

©The Education Center, Inc.

ANYTIME

Color Explosion

Materials:
(for one project)

coffee filter
sheet of 9" x 12" colored
   construction paper
black water-based marker
bowl of water
green marker
glue

1.

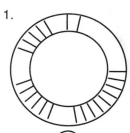

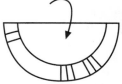

2.

3.

Preparation Hints:

1. Purchase coffee filters.

Student Steps:

Session 1:
1. Fold the coffee filter in half three times (see the illustrations for Step 1).
2. Use the black marker to draw a line on both sides of the folded filter (see the illustration for Step 2).
3. Place the point of the filter into the water up to the black line and watch the colors emerge.
4. Unfold the filter and allow it to dry.

Session 2:
1. Glue the filter to a piece of construction paper; then use the green marker to add a stem and leaves.

Finishing Touches:

1. Try some absorbency experiments with other types of paper.

*Gloria J. Barrow—Gr. K,
Dundee Elementary School,
Dundee, FL*

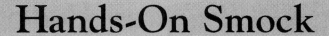

Hands-On Smock

Materials:
(for one project)

oversized white T-shirt
fabric paint (various colors)
disposable wipes
disposable pie tins

Preparation Hints:

1. Gather oversized T-shirts, fabric paint, and disposable wipes.
2. Collect several pie tins and pour a different color of paint into each.

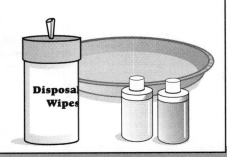

Student Steps:

1. Place a hand into one color of paint.
2. Press the hand on the T-shirt to make a print.
3. Clean the hand with a disposable wipe.
4. Repeat Steps 1, 2, and 3 using different colors of paint and a clean disposable wipe.
5. Allow the T-shirt to dry overnight.

Finishing Touches:

1. Have children wear as smocks during art and cooking activities.

Adapted from an idea by Tracy Stewart—Gr. 1, Southern Academy, Greensboro, AL

ANYTIME

Handy Family Puppet

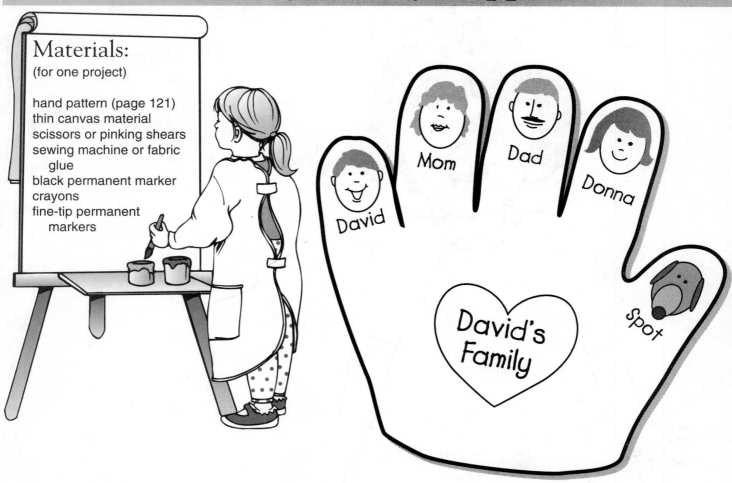

Materials:
(for one project)

hand pattern (page 121)
thin canvas material
scissors or pinking shears
sewing machine or fabric
   glue
black permanent marker
crayons
fine-tip permanent
   markers

David
Mom
Dad
Donna
Spot
David's
Family

Preparation Hints:

1. Collect material and obtain fabric glue if needed.
2. Use the hand pattern to cut hand shapes from canvas (two per child).
3. Sew or glue the edge of each pair of hands, leaving the wrist edge open.
4. Use the black marker to draw an oval on each finger.

Student Steps:

1. Draw one family member's face on each oval. First use a crayon to shade the oval with the appropriate skin color. Then draw the features with the fine-tip markers.
2. Write each family member's name beneath each oval.

Finishing Touches:

1. Label each child's puppet with her name as shown.
2. Have the children use the puppets to introduce their families to classmates.

*Carol A. Jasinski,
Preschool Special Education,
Buffalo Hearing And Speech Center,
Buffalo, NY*

©The Education Center, Inc.

ANYTIME

Tire Tracks

Materials:
(for one project)

sheet of 9" x 12" construction paper
several paper plates
tempera paint (various colors)
toy cars and trucks with different-sized wheels
newspaper

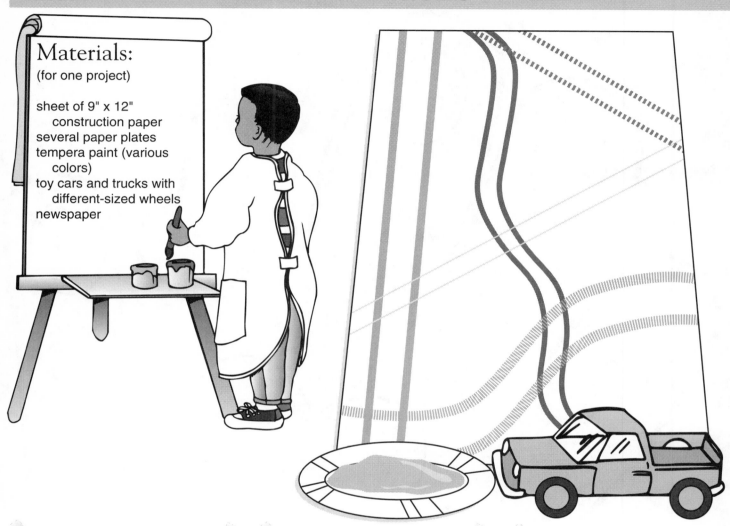

Preparation Hints:

1. Purchase paper plates.
2. Collect newspaper, toy cars, and trucks.
3. Pour a different color of paint onto each paper plate.

Student Steps:

1. Cover the work surface with newspaper.
2. Roll a toy car or truck through one color of paint.
3. Roll the toy across the construction paper.
4. Repeat Steps 2 and 3 using different cars or trucks and different paint colors.
5. Allow the paint to dry.

Finishing Touches:

1. Display the finished pictures on a bulletin board titled "Way To Go!"
2. Let youngsters guess which vehicles made the tracks in each picture.

*Anne M. Cromwell-Gapp—Gr. Pre-K,
Keene Day Care Center,
Keene, NH*

Icy Images

Materials:
(for one project)

sheet of 9" x 12" white
    construction paper
ice cube trays
bowls of water
food coloring
craft sticks

Preparation Hints:

1. Pour one color of food coloring into each bowl of water.
2. Pour the colored water into ice cube trays.
3. Place a craft stick in each cube section and freeze overnight.
4. Remove the cubes from the trays just before using.

Student Steps:

1. Hold the cubes by the craft-stick handles and paint designs on the white construction paper.

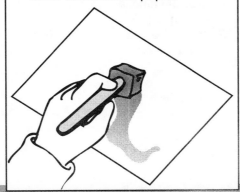

Finishing Touches:

1. Display the finished projects on a bulletin board titled "Cool Art."

*Anne M. Cromwell-Gapp—Gr. Pre-K,
Keene Day Care Center,
Keene, NH*

ANYTIME

Dino-Hat

Materials:

(for one project)

dinosaur pattern (pages
   125 and 126)
sheet of 9" x 12"
   white construction
   paper
24" piece of sentence strip
crayons
scissors
glue
stapler

Preparation Hints:

1. Cut sentence-strip pieces.
2. Duplicate a dinosaur pattern
   on construction paper for each
   child.

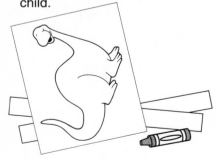

Student Steps:

1. Color and cut out the dinosaur
   pattern.
2. Glue the dinosaur to the
   sentence strip.
3. Staple the ends of the sentence
   strip together.

Finishing Touches:

1. Declare a "dinosaur day" and
   allow your children to wear their
   Dino-Hats to celebrate.
2. Have the children wear their hats
   and walk like dinosaurs in a fun
   dinosaur parade.

Dinosaur Pattern

©The Education Center, Inc.

Creative Cut-And-Paste

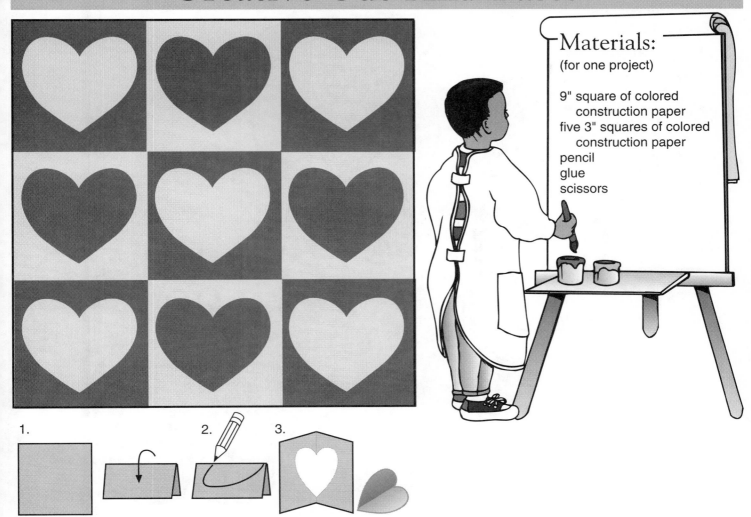

Materials:

(for one project)

9" square of colored
   construction paper
five 3" squares of colored
   construction paper
pencil
glue
scissors

1.   2.   3.

Preparation Hints:

1. Cut one color of construction paper into nine-inch squares.
2. Choose a different color of construction paper and cut into three-inch squares.

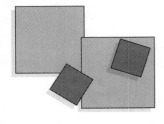

Student Steps:

1. Fold each three-inch square in half.
2. On the fold of each three-inch square, draw the same shape (see the illustration for Step 2).
3. Cut out each shape on the outline and set aside the cutouts.
4. Unfold the squares to reveal the design.
5. Glue a three-inch square in each corner of the nine-inch square.

6. Glue the remaining three-inch square in the center.
7. Glue a reserved cut out shape in each of the remaining four spaces. (There will be one shape left over.)

Finishing Touches:

1. Create a colorful display with the finished artwork.
2. Or cover with clear adhesive vinyl to make placemats.

*Karen Saner—Grs. K & 1,
Burns Elementary School,
Burns, KS*

Paper-Plate Pal

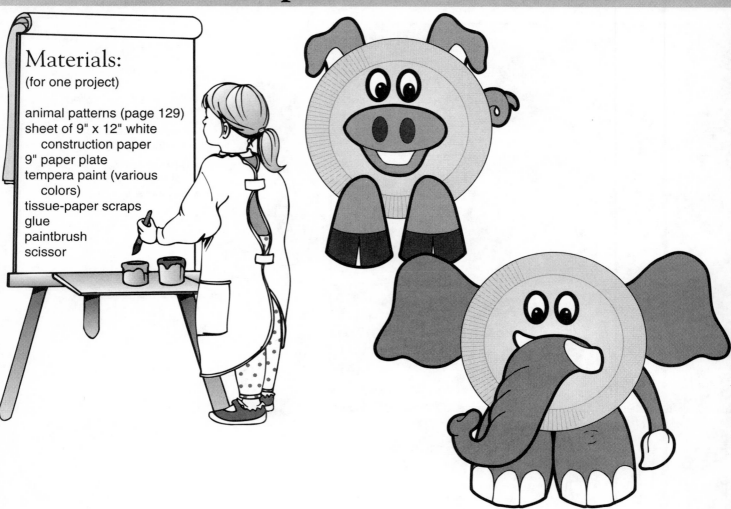

Materials:
(for one project)

animal patterns (page 129)
sheet of 9" x 12" white
   construction paper
9" paper plate
tempera paint (various
   colors)
tissue-paper scraps
glue
paintbrush
scissor

Preparation Hints:

1. Purchase paper plates.
2. Duplicate the animal patterns on white construction paper for each child.

Student Steps:

Session 1:
1. Choose an animal to make and paint the appropriate pattern pieces.
2. Paint the paper plate the appropriate color.
3. Allow the pattern pieces and plate to dry.

Session 2:
1. Cut out the pattern pieces and glue them to the plate as shown.
2. Cut and glue on tissue-paper scraps to add details.

Finishing Touches:

1. Display the finished animals on a bulletin board titled "Creative Creatures."

Debra Damiano,
Gr. K: Special Education,
Ash Street Center,
Forest Park, GA

ANYTIME

Detergent-Box Castle

Materials:
(for one project)

empty laundry-detergent box
2" squares of gray construction paper
2 empty bathroom-tissue rolls
construction-paper scraps
craft stick
glue
scissors

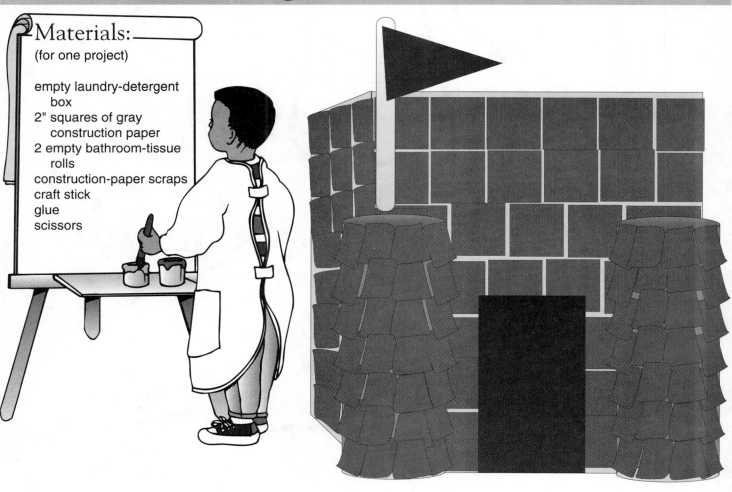

Preparation Hints:

1. Collect craft sticks.
2. Collect laundry-detergent boxes and bathroom-tissue rolls.
3. Cut a square in the side of each box.
4. Cut gray construction paper into two-inch squares.

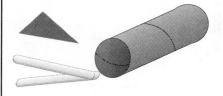

Student Steps:

1. Completely cover the box and tissue rolls by gluing on construction-paper squares.
2. Glue the rolls to the box as shown.
3. Cut a triangle from a construction-paper scrap and glue it to the craft stick to make a flag.
4. Glue the craft stick to the box to complete the castle.

Finishing Touches:

1. Display the castles in the classroom with the title "Castle Creations."

Jayne M. Gammons—Grs. K & 1, Oak Grove School, Durham, NC

ANYTIME 130

Ready, Aim, Squirt!

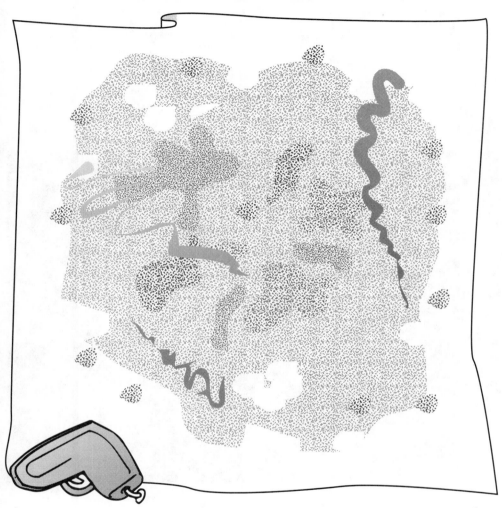

Materials:
(for one project)

large piece of plain fabric
diluted tempera paint
(various colors)
squirt guns

Preparation Hints:

1. Bring in a large piece of fabric and collect squirt guns from students.
2. Dilute several colors of tempera.
3. Fill each squirt gun with a different color of diluted paint.
4. Drape the fabric over an outside fence.

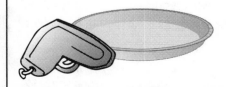

Student Steps:

1. Squirt the fabric with various colors of tempera paint.
2. Allow the paint to dry.

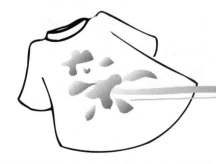

Finishing Touches:

1. Trim the edges of the fabric to fit on a bulletin board as a colorful background.
2. As a variation, try this technique on solid-colored T-shirts. Have children wear the T-shirts on fieldtrip days to help identify your class.

ANYTIME

Sensational Star

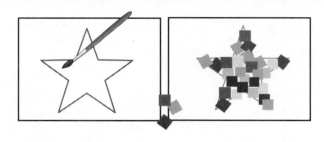

Materials:
(for one project)

star pattern (page 133)
sheet of 9" x 12" white
    construction paper
sheet of 9" x 12" black
    construction paper
1" tissue-paper squares
    (various colors)
crayon
diluted glue
paintbrush
scissors

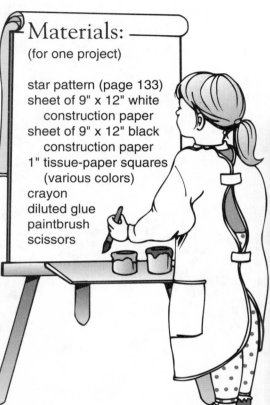

Preparation Hints:

1. Duplicate a star pattern on white construction paper for each child.
2. Dilute some white glue.
3. Cut tissue paper into squares.

Student Steps:

Session 1:
1. Cut out the star pattern.
2. Brush a coat of diluted glue over the entire star.
3. Press tissue-paper squares on the glue, overlapping edges and completely covering the star.
4. Allow the glue to dry.

Session 2:
1. Trim the excess tissue paper from around the edges.

2. Glue the star (colored side up) to the black construction paper.
3. Brush a final coat of glue over the star and allow to dry.

Finishing Touches:

1. Display the finished pictures in your reading corner. Have children enjoy their artwork while you read Eric Carle's book *Draw Me A Star*.

Kristine Stafira—Gr. K,
All Saints School,
Manassas, VA

ANYTIME

 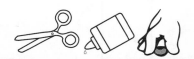

Birthday Crown

Materials:
(for one project)

crown pattern (page 135)
sheet of 9" x 12" colored
    construction paper
24" piece of sentence strip
decorative items such as:
    glitter, plastic jewels,
    sequins, fabric scraps
marker
glue
scissors
stapler

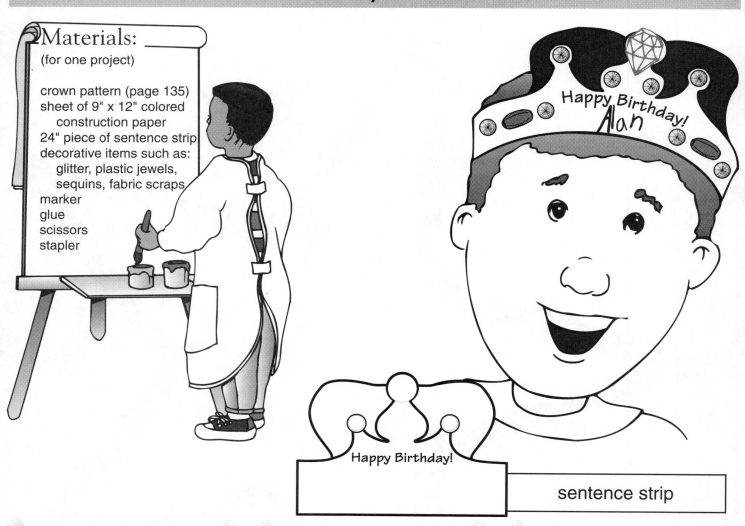

Happy Birthday!

sentence strip

Preparation Hints:

1. Collect decorative items.
2. Duplicate a crown pattern on colored construction paper for each child.

Student Steps:

1. Cut out the crown pattern.
2. Decorate the crown by gluing on the desired decorative items.
3. Write your name on the crown with a marker.
4. Staple a sentence strip to one end of the crown.

Finishing Touches:

1. Fit each child's crown to her head and staple the ends. Have children wear their crowns as everyone sings "Happy Birthday To You."
2. Then store the crowns away. Present each child with her crown to wear all day on her birthday as a special treat!

*Jayne M. Gammons—Grs. K & 1,
Oak Grove School,
Durham, NC*

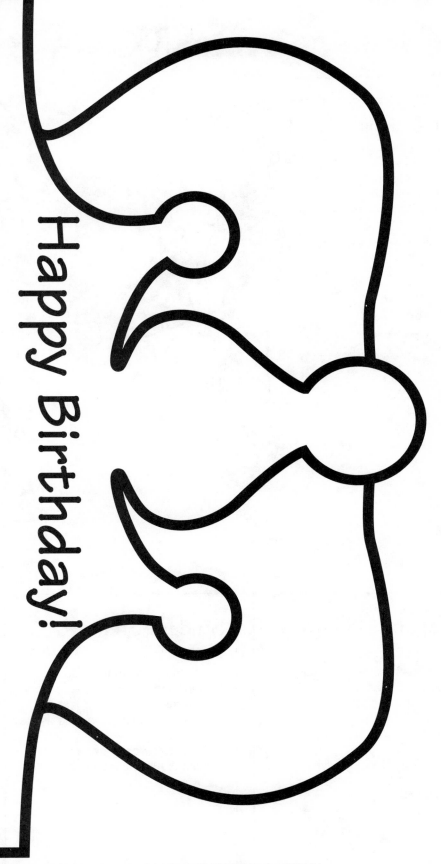

Happy Birthday!

©The Education Center, Inc.

Animal On A Roll

Materials:
(for one project)

farm animal patterns
   (pages 137–138)
empty bathroom-tissue roll
sheet of 9" x 12"
   construction paper
crayons
glue
scissors

Preparation Hints:

1. Collect bathroom-tissue rolls.
2. Duplicate the animal patterns on construction paper.

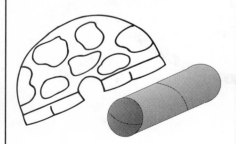

Student Steps:

1. Choose an animal shape.
2. Color and cut out the necessary patterns.
3. Glue the cover around the tissue roll.
4. Glue on the body parts for your animal. Allow the glue to dry.

Finishing Touches:

1. Create a farm scene with a barn cut from red construction paper, add hay, then display the finished animals.

Debra Damiano,
Gr. K: Special Education,
Ash Street Center,
Forest Park, GA

ANYTIME

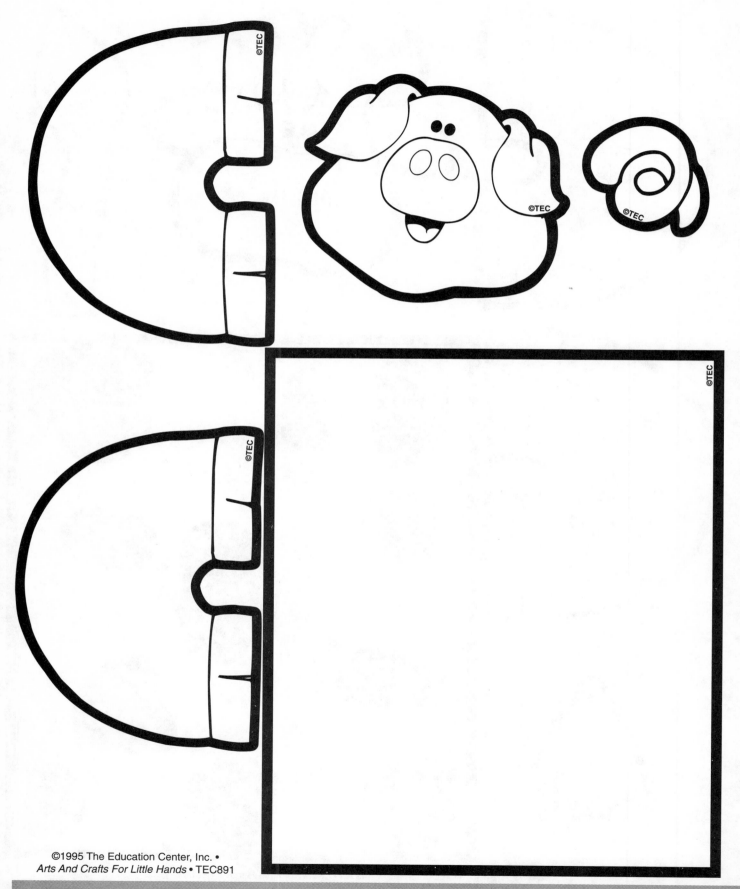

Big Building Blocks

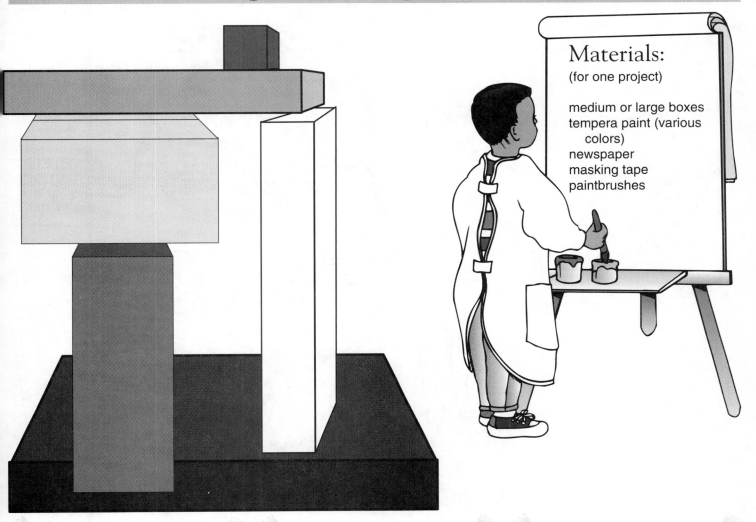

Materials:
(for one project)

medium or large boxes
tempera paint (various
  colors)
newspaper
masking tape
paintbrushes

Preparation Hints:

1. Collect boxes and newspaper.

Student Steps:

1. Cover the work area with newspaper.
2. Seal a box closed with masking tape.
3. Paint the box with one color of paint and allow to dry.
4. Repeat Steps 2 and 3 with other boxes and colors.

Finishing Touches:

1. Have children use the finished boxes as giant building blocks.

*Andrea Esposito—Gr. Pre-K,
VA/YMCA Child Care Center,
Brooklyn, NY*

"Snackmat"

Materials:
(for one project)

12" x 18" sheet of white
   construction paper
fruits and vegetables (cut
   in half)
tempera paint (various
   colors)
clear adhesive vinyl
black crayon
paintbrushes

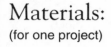

Gina's Mat

Stephen's Mat

Preparation Hints:

1. Purchase clear adhesive vinyl
   and collect several different fruits
   and vegetables.
2. Cut fruits and vegetables into
   halves.

Student Steps:

1. Print your name on the paper
   with a black crayon.
2. Paint the flat side of a fruit or
   vegetable half.
3. Press the painted side on the
   construction paper.
4. Repeat Steps 1 and 2 with other
   fruits and vegetables and other
   paint colors.
5. Allow the paint to dry.

Finishing Touches:

1. Cover each child's paper with
   clear adhesive vinyl.
2. Have the students use the
   placemats at snacktime.
3. As a variation for St. Patrick's
   Day, have the class try potato-
   printing on the placemats.

Bonny Bonnet

Materials:

(for one project)

9" paper plate
two 12" lengths of yarn
decorative items such as:
    yarn, ribbon, paper
    scraps, stickers, fabric
    scraps, lace, buttons
tempera paint (various
    colors)
glue
paintbrush
hole puncher
newspaper

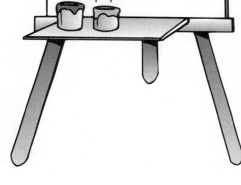

Preparation Hints:

1. Collect paper plates, decorative items, and newspaper.
2. Cut yarn into lengths.
3. Pour paint into small containers.

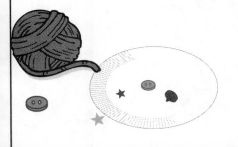

Student Steps:

Session 1:
1. Cover the work area with newspaper.
2. Paint the bottom side of the paper plate.
3. Allow the paint to dry.

Session 2:
1. Punch a hole about one inch from the edge on opposite sides of the paper plate.
2. Thread a length of yarn through each hole and tie a knot to secure it.

3. Glue on the desired decorative items. (The more, the better!)

Finishing Touches:

1. Place each child's hat on his head and tie the yarn into a bow under his chin. Let students wear their hats while you read *Jennie's Hat* by Ezra Jack Keats.

ANYTIME

Fluffy Fish

Materials:
(for one project)

fish patterns (page 143)
sheet of 9" x 12" colored
   construction paper
two 9" paper plates
1" tissue-paper squares
glue
scissors
stapler

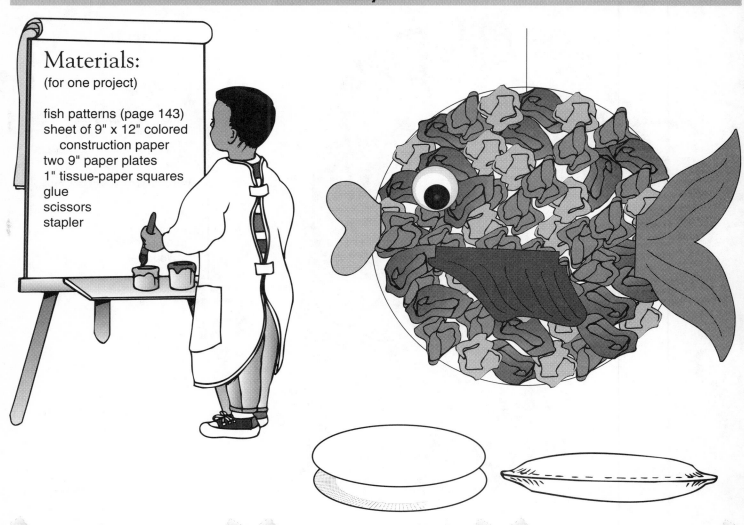

Preparation Hints:

1. Obtain paper plates.
2. Duplicate the fish patterns on colored construction paper for each child.
3. Cut tissue paper into squares.

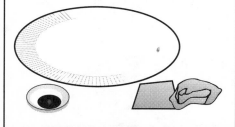

Student Steps:

Session 1:
1. Invert one paper plate on top of the other and staple the edges as shown.
2. Crumple squares of tissue paper and glue them to the plates, completely covering both sides. Allow the glue to dry.

Session 2:
1. Cut out the fish eyes, fins, and tail.
2. Glue on the fish features. Allow the glue to dry.

Finishing Touches:

1. Turn your classroom into an aquarium by suspending the completed fish from the ceiling with lengths of yarn.
2. Gather children together to hear *Fish Is Fish* by Leo Lionni.

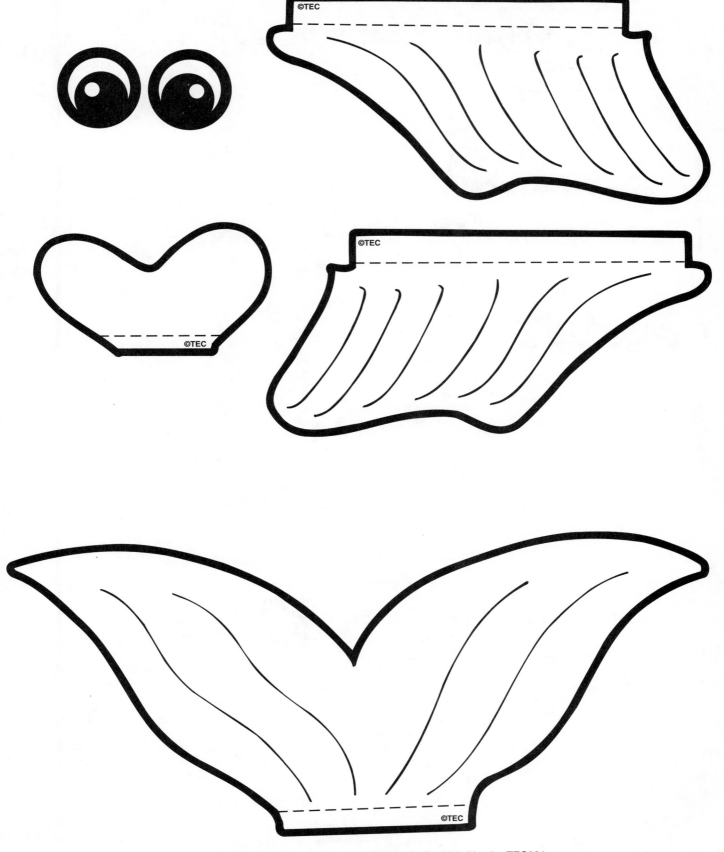

©TEC

©TEC

©TEC

©TEC

©1995 The Education Center, Inc. • *Arts And Crafts For Little Hands* • TEC891

ANYTIME

Dazzling Dream Catcher

Materials:
(for one project)

waxed paper
5 lengths of yarn (24" each)
disposable pie pan
glitter
diluted glue

Preparation Hints:

1. Purchase multicolored glitter if necessary.
2. Cut yarn into lengths.
3. Dilute some white glue and pour into a disposable pie pan.

Student Steps:

Session 1:
1. Spread a sheet of waxed paper over the work surface.
2. Soak a length of yarn in diluted glue.
3. Shape the yarn into a circle on the waxed paper, making sure the ends overlap.
4. Soak three more lengths of yarn and arrange them inside the circle in a weblike design. Make sure the ends of the yarn pieces touch the outer circle.
5. Sprinkle the yarn with glitter and allow to dry.

Session 2:
1. Remove the hardened design from the waxed paper and tie the remaining length of yarn to the outer circle.

Finishing Touches:

1. Decorate your classroom by suspending the dream catchers in front of the windows.

Jennifer Fry,
Kyrene School District,
Chandler, AZ

Mini Critter

Materials:
(for one project)

single segment of a
   cardboard egg carton
tempera paint
1/2 sheet of 9" x 12" white
   construction paper
colored markers or crayons
glue
paintbrush
scissors

Preparation Hints:

1. Collect and cut apart egg cartons.
2. Cut white construction paper into half sheets.

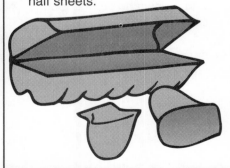

Student Steps:

1. Decide what kind of critter to make.
2. Paint the outside of the egg carton segment as desired.
3. Draw features for your animal on white construction paper.
4. Cut out the features and glue them to the egg carton segment.

Finishing Touches:

1. Read *Do You Want To Be My Friend?* by Eric Carle; then display the finished critters on a table with the book.

Beth Schimmel—Gr. Pre-K,
Blue Ridge Elementary School,
Pinetop, AZ

ANYTIME

Spaghetti Tree

Materials:

(for one project)

spaghetti noodles (cooked)
green food coloring
cinnamon-spiced tea leaves
sheet of 9" x 12"
    construction paper
green and brown markers
glue

Preparation Hints:

1. Purchase spaghetti noodles and cinnamon-spiced tea leaves.
2. Cook and drain the spaghetti and place in a bowl. Mix in green food coloring and let sit until the color is absorbed.

Student Steps:

1. Use the markers to draw a tree outline on the construction paper.
2. Squeeze glue over the top section of the tree and press on spaghetti noodles to make leaves.
3. Spread a coat of glue over the tree trunk and sprinkle on tea leaves.
4. Shake off the excess tea and allow to dry.

Finishing Touches:

1. Display the finished projects on a bulletin board titled " 'Spaghet-tea' Trees."
2. For fall trees, color the spaghetti with yellow and orange food coloring.

*Beth Schimmel—Gr. Pre-K,
Blue Ridge Elementary School,
Pinetop, AZ*

Cinnamon Circus Animal

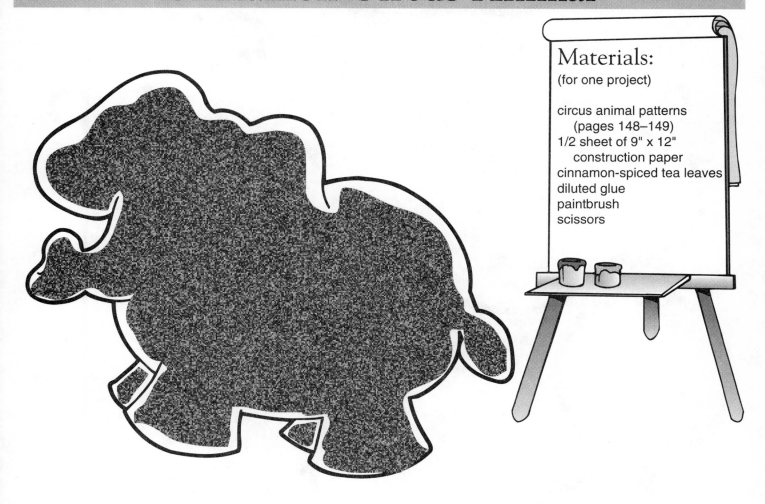

Materials:
(for one project)

circus animal patterns
(pages 148–149)
1/2 sheet of 9" x 12"
construction paper
cinnamon-spiced tea leaves
diluted glue
paintbrush
scissors

Preparation Hints:

1. Purchase cinnamon-spiced tea leaves.
2. Duplicate several copies of the circus animal patterns on construction paper.
3. Dilute some white glue.

Student Steps:

1. Choose and cut out an animal pattern.
2. Brush a coat of diluted glue on the cutout and sprinkle on tea leaves.
3. Shake off the excess tea and allow to dry.

Finishing Touches:

1. Display the finished animals on a bulletin board titled "Cinnamon Circus."
2. Gather children together to hear *Circus* by Lois Ehlert or *Ernest And Celestine At The Circus* by Gabrielle Vincent.

Beth Schimmel—Gr. Pre-K, Blue Ridge Elementary School, Pinetop, AZ

ANYTIME

©The Education Center, Inc.

©The Education Center, Inc.

Season Mobile

Materials:
(for one project)

seasonal patterns (pages 151–152)
three 9" paper plates
three 2" lengths of yarn
two 5" lengths of yarn
8 1/2" x 11" tagboard
construction paper
tempera paint and a brush
colored glue and glitter
scissors
stapler

Preparation Hints:

1. Gather paper plates, colored glue, and glitter.
2. Duplicate the seasonal patterns on tagboard and cut out for use as templates.
3. Punch a hole in the center of each plate as a starting point for cutting. (Or, if desired, cut out the centers for younger students.)
4. Cut yarn into lengths.

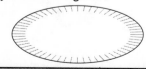

Student Steps:

Session 1:
1. Cut out the center of each paper plate.
2. Paint the rim of each plate.
3. Trace and cut out three seasonal patterns from construction paper.
4. Decorate the cutouts with colored glue and glitter. Allow to dry.

Session 2:
1. Staple a two-inch length of yarn to each cutout and suspend in the center of paper plates as shown.
2. Connect the three plates with the five-inch lengths of yarn as shown.

Finishing Touches:

1. Suspend the mobiles from your classroom ceiling for seasonal flair.
2. Have children create new mobiles for each season.

*Karen Saner—Grs. K & 1,
Burns Elementary School,
Burns, KS*

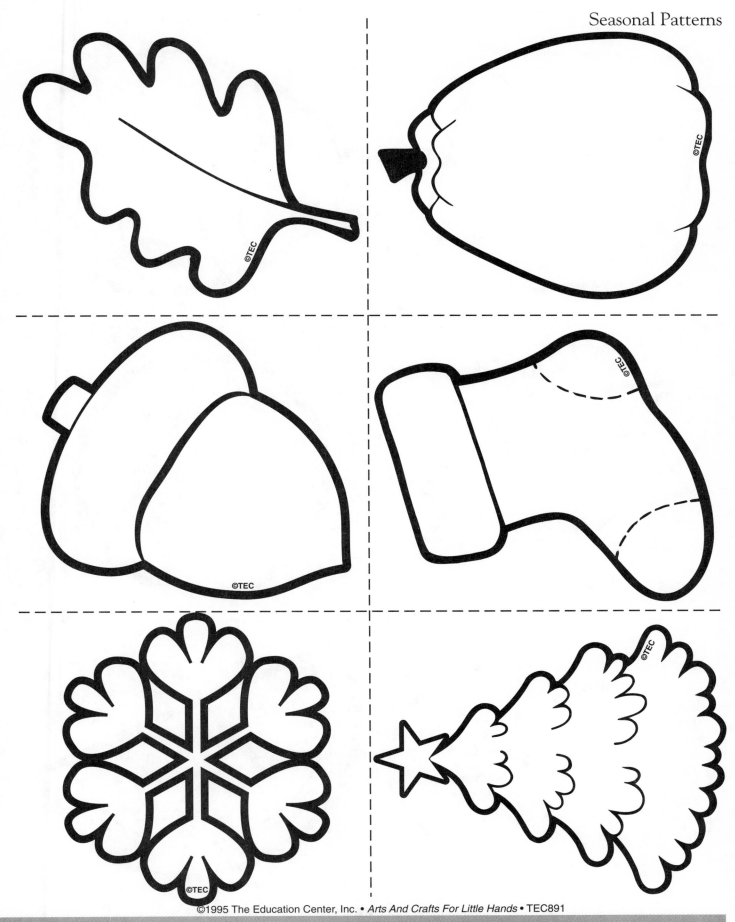

ANYTIME

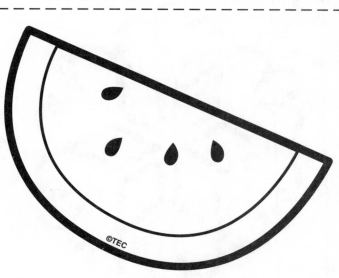

Cereal Signature

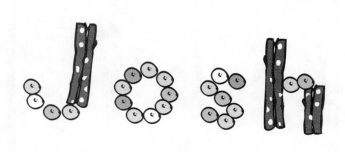

Materials:
(for one project)

12" x 18" sheet of white
    construction paper
pretzel sticks
o-shaped cereal
marker
glue

Preparation Hints:

1. Purchase pretzel sticks and
   o-shaped cereal.
2. Use the marker to write each
   child's name in large block
   letters on a sheet of 12" x 18"
   white paper.

Student Steps:

1. Squeeze a trail of glue over the
   first letter in your name.
2. Press pretzel sticks to the
   straight lines in the letter. Cover
   the curved parts of the letter with
   o-shaped cereal as shown.
3. Glue the pretzels and o-shaped
   cereal to the other letters in your
   name.
4. Allow the glue to dry.

Finishing Touches:

1. Enjoy a snack of pretzels and
   dry cereal with your students
   while admiring the finished
   artwork!
2. Display the projects in your
   writing center for children's
   reference when writing each
   others' names.

ANYTIME

Family Faces

Materials:
(for one project)

paper cupcake liners
12" x 18" sheet of
   construction paper
crayons
glue

Preparation Hints:

1. Obtain cupcake liners.

Student Steps:

1. On each cupcake liner, draw a
   member of your family (including
   you).
2. Label each liner with the
   person's name.
3. Draw and color a large tree on
   the construction paper.
4. Glue the cupcake liners to the
   tree as shown and allow to dry.

Finishing Touches:

1. Display the finished projects on a
   bulletin board titled "A Forest Of
   Family Trees."

Beth Schimmel—Gr. Pre-K,
Blue Ridge Elementary School,
Pinetop, AZ

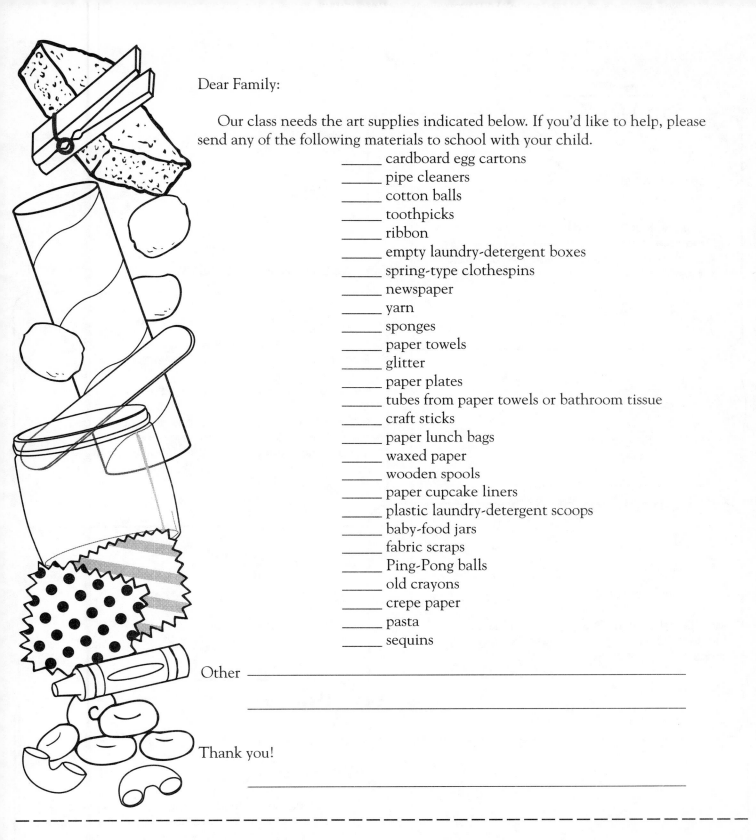

Dear Family:

Our class needs the art supplies indicated below. If you'd like to help, please send any of the following materials to school with your child.

_____ cardboard egg cartons
_____ pipe cleaners
_____ cotton balls
_____ toothpicks
_____ ribbon
_____ empty laundry-detergent boxes
_____ spring-type clothespins
_____ newspaper
_____ yarn
_____ sponges
_____ paper towels
_____ glitter
_____ paper plates
_____ tubes from paper towels or bathroom tissue
_____ craft sticks
_____ paper lunch bags
_____ waxed paper
_____ wooden spools
_____ paper cupcake liners
_____ plastic laundry-detergent scoops
_____ baby-food jars
_____ fabric scraps
_____ Ping-Pong balls
_____ old crayons
_____ crepe paper
_____ pasta
_____ sequins

Other _____

_____

Thank you!

_____

- -

Note To Teacher: Before duplicating, check the items you need, add any others not on the list, and sign your name. Send home with students at the beginning of the year or anytime supplies are needed.

Recipes

Salt Dough

2 cups flour
1 cup salt
1 cup cold water
food coloring (optional)

Place the flour, salt, and water in a bowl and stir. Knead the mixture until it forms a smooth dough. Add more flour or water to reach the desired consistency. To add color to the dough, simply knead in food coloring.

Decorative Dye

1 container with lid
1 tablespoon rubbing alcohol
food coloring

Color rice, macaroni, or pasta with this easy dye recipe. In a small, tightly lidded container, put one tablespoon of rubbing alcohol and six drops of food coloring. Place the objects to be dyed into the mixture and secure the lid. Shake the container gently for one minute. Spread the dyed objects on paper towels to dry.

Bubble Mixture

1/4 cup dishwashing liquid
1/2 cup water
1 teaspoon sugar
food coloring (optional)

Mix the dishwashing liquid, water, and sugar together in a bowl. If color is desired, mix in a few drops of food coloring.

Baking Dough

4 tablespoons flour
1 tablespoon salt
2 tablespoons water

Your students can measure and mix this dough recipe on their own. Mix the ingredients together; then shape the dough or roll it out and cut with cookie cutters. Bake the dough at 350° for 1 to 1 1/2 hours. Finished products can be painted.

Techniques

Finicky Fingers

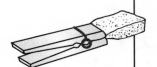

small square sponges
spring-type clothespins
tempera paint

This method helps children keep their fingers clean while sponge-painting. Clip a clothespin to each small sponge. Then hold the clothespin and dip the sponge into tempera paint. Use a different sponge and clothespin for each color of paint.

Suzanne Costner, Maryville, TN

Paper-Towel Painting

paper towels
tempera paint

Use this technique in place of sponge-painting. Crumple a paper towel and dip it into paint. Dab the paint on your paper to create the desired design. When you are finished, just throw the paper towel away!

*Karen Saner—Grs. K & 1,
Burns Elementary School,
Burns, KS*

Easy Foil Cutting

When using aluminum foil for art projects, use this tip for hassle-free cutting. Place the foil between two sheets of newspaper, draw the desired shape on the newspaper, then cut out the shape. Remove the newspaper and your crisply cut foil pattern is ready to go.

*Flo Spradlin—Gr. K,
Central Elementary School,
MS*

Paint Cup Cleanup

Paint cleanup will take only seconds with this clever idea. Place a plastic bag inside each paint cup that you will be using. Pour paint into each of the bags in the cups. When the paint has been used up, simply toss out the bag.

*Debbie Newsome—Gr. K,
Dolvin Elementary School,
Alpharetta, GA*

Crayon Chunks

Make use of old and broken crayon pieces by turning them into crayon chunks. Line each cup of a muffin pan with three paper cupcake liners. Peel the paper wrappings off all of the crayon pieces; then fill each of the muffin cups about half way with crayon pieces. (You can sort the pieces by color and/or mix several colors together as you like.) Place the muffin pan in a 250° oven for about 20 minutes until the crayon pieces have melted. When the crayons are cool, peel the liners from each crayon chunk and you've got big new crayons for little artists' hands.

*Fran Blaess—Gr. K,
Kennedy School,
Middletown, RI*

5...4...3 2...1...

_____'s
artwork is out
of this world!

Signed: _____   Date: _____

(teacher signature)

©The Education Center, Inc.

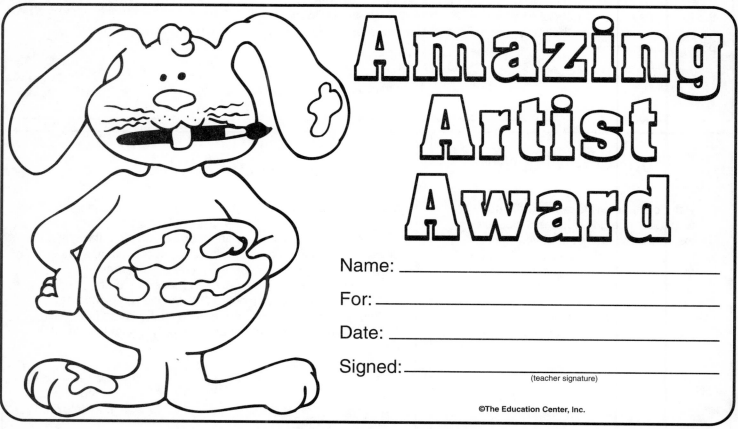

Amazing Artist Award

Name: _____

For: _____

Date: _____

Signed: _____

(teacher signature)

©The Education Center, Inc.

Index